SOCIOCRACY 3.0 - THE NOVEL

Note:
The fact that we use the male pronoun (he/his) throughout the text is
for ease of reading and in no way reflects an attitude of gender bias.

The co-creators of S3 — James Priest, Bernhard Bockelbrink and Liliana David —
have granted Jef Cumps a worldwide non-exclusive and non-transferable license to use text
and illustrations from "Sociocracy 3.0 - A Practical Guide" (www.sociocracy30.org) in this book.

This book was originally published as *Sociocratie 3.0 – De businessnovelle die het beste uit mens en organisatie haalt*, LannooCampus, 2018.

D/2019/45/463 – ISBN 978 94 014 6398 0 – NUR 800

Cover and interior design: Gert Degrande | De Witlofcompagnie
Illustrations: Jef Cumps

© Jef Cumps & Lannoo Publishers nv, Tielt, 2019.

LannooCampus Publishers is a subsidiary of Lannoo Publishers,
the book and multimedia division of Lannoo Publishers nv.

LannooCampus Publishers
Vaartkom 41 bus 01.02
3000 Leuven
Belgium
www.lannoocampus.be
www.lannoocampus.com

P.O. Box 23202
1100 DS Amsterdam
Netherlands
www.lannoocampus.nl

JEF CUMPS

Unleash
the Full Potential
of People and Organizations

SOCIOCRACY 3.0
THE NOVEL

LANNOO
CAMPUS

FOREWORD

I first met Jef in spring 2015, when he attended an S3 workshop that Lili David and I ran. S3 was five months old at the time. I particularly remember Jef — he has an inquisitive demeanor and asked probing questions as we talked after the session. He foresaw that S3 patterns were probably going to prove useful in enabling an agile mindset to permeate throughout an entire organization.

That was back in the early days when we were still figuring how to even talk about S3. Things have come a long way since then. And that also applies to Jef, who, besides being one of the finest teachers and coaches I have ever met, has developed a thorough grasp of S3.

Thanks to Jef, by the spring of 2016 we'd run the first S3 introduction course in Belgium. We hooked up in Lisbon soon after, and Jef told me about his idea for a book. He already had a pretty good idea of the story line as he introduced me to Chris, Bernie and some of the other characters you're going to meet. I was intrigued because many of them seemed familiar to me. They probably will to you too!

Jef wanted to portray a story that would give people practical, realistic insights into how to pull in patterns from S3, on an as-needed basis and at a pace that they could decide on themselves. He wanted to show, step-by-step, how an entire organization could radically improve its capacity to navigate complexity, increase the flow of value and harness the creative potential, passion and engagement of all.

I believe he has succeeded!

This book is jam-packed with useful insights and perspectives that will help members of any organization enjoy greater satisfaction and effectiveness at work. Jef has a highly developed capacity for transmitting useful wisdom in a simple and digestible way. This story of transformation reveals how a typical tech company hit a wall and made it through, to both survive and thrive. It's a must-read for anyone interested in growing more humane, innovative and resilient organizations. Organizations that we can proudly pass on to our children as an inspiration for how they too can successfully work together and thrive.

James Priest, co-creator and developer of Sociocracy 3.0

1

PAUL'S QUESTION

My phone rings. The name of Paul, our CEO, appears on the screen.

He gets straight to the point: "Chris, I have something important to discuss with you. Can you meet me in the lobby at 6.30 this evening?"

"Okay, Paul. What's going on?"

"I'll tell you tonight, but the future of Human Resources Solutions could depend on it. So please don't tell anyone about our meeting yet," he says, and hangs up.

I stare at my phone wondering what this is all about. Why would he want to talk to me? It must be serious as he doesn't usually use the full name of our company.

It probably has something to do with the new version of our product, a software package for HR departments. Version 4.0 of this software should have been ready months ago. But various problems, especially regarding testing and integration of components, have prevented us from getting there. Worse, we haven't even managed to get version 4.0 sufficiently stable. This is why we missed the opportunity to present it at an important international fair last week.

Still, I don't understand why Paul wants to speak to me. The mobile applications work perfectly and were ready on time. Could there be something else going wrong in my department?

I keep thinking about the phone call for the rest of the afternoon, so I'm happy when 6.30 finally arrives. When I get to the lobby, Paul is already waiting for me. He invites me outside for a walk and wastes no time: "Chris, you've seen HRS and our product grow from the start and that's why I want to tell you something in confidence. May I?"

"Sure, Paul," I say.

Paul hesitates as he searches for the right words.

"I'm just going to tell it like it is," he says. "I'm thinking about stepping down as CEO. I'm afraid that I'm no longer the right man in the right place."

"Gosh, Paul," I respond, "I didn't see this coming."

"No, I understand," he replies. "I probably should have talked about it before, but I didn't want to create any anxiety. I thought I could figure it out myself."

I look at Paul quizzically.

"We've grown a lot in recent years, you know that. In the past, I knew everyone personally, and I knew what was going on in the entire company. But that hasn't been the case for a while now. We've been creating departments, management positions and processes to support our growth. But despite all the weekly reports and monthly performance indicators, I've lost control."

Paul sighs. His gaze is both serious and sad. I've never seen him so helpless.

"Tell me more, Paul," I encourage him.

"I've been noticing for some time that we're slower to make decisions than before and that people talk less to each other, at least about the things that matter. In the beginning, when we built our first product with a few dozen people, everyone knew everyone. We knew who was doing what, what the problems were and how we could help each other. But now we seem to be losing that team spirit bit by bit. Walls are being built between departments, people withhold information for fear of being blamed for mistakes, and management is playing political games — as if everyone is protecting his own position and his own team."

"Yes, I recognize that," I say carefully.

"That makes us slow and heavy, Chris. We respond less quickly and flexibly to customer inquiries. And we missed the deadline to be able to present our new product internationally, which is why the board of directors is asking me for a justification."

He continues: "Which makes sense, given that the future of the company depends on the sales of the new version of our product. If we can't meet the expectations of our investors and the market, the whole story stops right here."

I understand what Paul is saying, but I'm still not quite sure why it's me walking beside him right now.

"I don't think I can do this, Chris. Even though I've done what I could in recent years, it hasn't been enough. I've been thinking about this a lot over the last few weeks and I think it's time for a new captain. Someone who can pull this ship back on track."

Paul stops and turns to me.

"There's a board meeting planned for Wednesday, when I will resign from my position as CEO. And I'll take responsibility for that missed deadline. This will temporarily reassure the board of directors and the investors and will give the new CEO time to speed up."

"The new CEO?" I stammer. What does he mean?

"Chris, I want to ask you to take my place. I realize that you were not expecting this question at all, but I've thought about it long and hard. You're the only one in the organization who has managed to preserve the atmosphere, cooperation and quality of the past in his department. Your mobile applications do what they are supposed to do and they are almost always ready on time. Your people seem to be happy, and you usually walk through the company with a smile. I don't know exactly how you do it, but I believe in you, Chris. You can save this company."

I'm perplexed, and for a moment I think he's joking. Should I become CEO of HRS, a listed company with 160 employees? That's impossible!

Paul sees the panic in my eyes and smiles, though he still looks sad.

"I mean it, Chris. I believe you can bring in the necessary change. You don't have to accept my offer right away, but I would appreciate it if you gave it

some serious thought. I expect your answer by Wednesday morning, before
I go to the board, okay?"

I nod, but I don't know what to say. Wednesday? That's only five days from
now!

2

KATE

"So, what are you going to do?" my wife Kate asks curiously after I've finished telling her about my conversation with Paul.

"Oh, becoming CEO isn't for me," I reply. "I really don't have the talent for playing the big boss, bearing all the responsibility and constantly having to play politics."

Kate looks at me with a frown, so I quickly continue: "I'm not as good at all in this as Paul. He's brilliant. He knows exactly what he wants and how he has to play the management team and our partners to reach his goals. And he has an extremely large network."

"Well, apparently whatever Paul is doing isn't working after all," Kate counters. "But, of course, if that's how you think about it, you really shouldn't do it."

She walks into the living room and leaves me behind, perplexed.

I follow her and ask her: "What do you mean? So you also think that I'm not capable of being the CEO?"

"It depends, sweetheart," she answers.

She asks me to sit down on the couch next to her.

"If you believe that a CEO has to be bossy and play politics," she says, "then this job is definitely not for you. But wouldn't that same strategy be expected of a line manager in your position?"

"Probably," I admit.

"But that's not how you function, Chris. You're always so proud of how your teams organize themselves without you having to worry about it. The members of your department don't look at you as their boss, but more as one of their peers. And that's because you don't position yourself as their superior, but as someone who wants to achieve certain goals with them. Someone they can trust and who's open and honest."

Kate looks at me.

"Think about when you're happiest arriving home at night, Chris. Not when you've done something important, but whenever a team has come up with a particular insight or started an interesting experiment. Or when you see that one of your people is going through a phase of major growth. That's your leadership style. And successfully so. What's more, you even have time to help with the programming here and there."

I nod. That's true. Since I joined the company, I've done my best to work in an "agile" way within my department. Agile is a philosophy in which small, self-organizing teams deliver working parts of a product on a regular basis instead of one huge piece of work at the end. This allows us to get early and continuous feedback from our clients and build the most valuable products. And we can easily and cheaply respond to insights and changes as we go along.

DEFINITION

Agile is a mindset in which small, self-organizing teams regularly deliver working increments of a product, thereby maximizing customer value.

"Wouldn't it be amazing to lead an entire organization that way?" Kate challenges me. "Imagine the whole of HRS working the way your team does these days. Wouldn't that be fantastic?"

"Kate, the way I work in my small department would never work on that level," I exclaim, justifying my decision. "Organizations don't work that way. On that level, you need hierarchy and politics. You can't be transparent and trust everyone just like that. It would all go haywire."

"That's a shame," Kate sighs.

"Well, unfortunately, that's the way it is," I say.

"That's not what I mean."

I look at her in surprise.

"I mean, I think it's a shame that you accept this so readily. In the past you wouldn't have. Do you remember when we were students and you had it out with the director over the way he was running the university? You didn't give up until things really changed."

I grin. Those were fantastic times indeed.

"And you didn't do all that for yourself, Chris. You stood up for other students who were disadvantaged. You wanted to change the world, and you went for it. You didn't care whether you ran into established systems."

She takes a breath and continues: "It's this rebellious side of you that I'm missing in your decision to not become CEO. You accept things the way they are, even though deep down you know that there are different and better approaches. You're already showing that with your own teams."

I want to counter her, but understand that she has a point.

"Do you think that I could save the company?" I ask her.

"I don't know, sweetheart," she answers. "But if you don't try, you'll never know."

I sigh, and begin to doubt my decision to refuse Paul's offer.

"I haven't the faintest idea how I would even begin," I say after a long pause. "There's so much that needs to be changed within HRS. I don't think the board will ever approve it."

"That last part you will only know for sure if you ask them," Kate suggests. She smiles and her eyes suddenly shine as she says: "Perhaps I even know a way to find out how to do all this."

3

BERNIE

The next morning I leave the house feeling both curious and skeptical. I'm on my way to see Bernie, someone Kate had met at a conference a while ago. Even though Bernie is retired, he still seems to be one of the key players at The Facts. The Facts is an organization that publishes honest, politically neutral news, unspoiled by corporate lobbies. According to Kate, they collaborate with dozens of journalists who work there either as volunteers or as paid employees. Kate didn't have all the details, but through her conversations with Bernie she did know that they've been working with small, self-organizing teams for years — without managers or a power hierarchy. She also knew that they had developed ways to continuously evaluate and improve themselves. Because Kate was so certain that Bernie could help me, she had called him yesterday evening, right after our conversation. He immediately agreed to meet up and share his experience with me.

Bernie looks younger than I had imagined, with an open face, clear eyes and a full head of grey curls. I would never have put him in his mid-sixties. He shakes my hand firmly and seems genuinely happy to meet me.

"So, you are the new CEO of HRS, Chris?" he welcomes me with a wink. "Come on in."

"Not really," I mutter. "I haven't decided anything yet."

"Of course not," Bernie laughs. "I'm teasing you. But I'm happy that you're considering it. Kate told me about your teams and your style as a manager. It's no small feat to run a whole company that way, but it is possible. At The Facts, we're living proof of that."

I've only just arrived and I'm already beginning to like Bernie. How crazy! He radiates gentleness and calmness while coming across as highly energetic and driven at the same time. He tells me more about The Facts and confirms that they are not using a traditional power hierarchy. The staff at The Facts organize themselves into small teams and take many decisions autonomously.

"Does that mean you are a completely flat organization, without any structure?" I interrupt him.

"No, not at all," Bernie laughs. "After all, what is a flat organization? We have a clear structure and clear agreements that govern how we act and what we do. This way, the power to make decisions and to influence what happens is distributed throughout the organization. A clear structure also helps to ensure that together we cover all the work necessary to keep the organization running smoothly."

We have a clear structure and clear agreements to let information and influence effectively flow to the right people.

I still don't fully understand how information and influence can be brought to the right people without a traditional power hierarchy, but Bernie goes on. He seems really enthusiastic about The Facts' way of working, just as Kate had said.

Bernie explains that all information and decisions are transparent, unless there is a good reason for confidentiality around something specific. This also means that everyone takes full responsibility for their part of the work without having to involve any managers.

I'm impressed, and I tell him what HRS does and that I'm in charge of the department that builds mobile applications for our software packages. Bernie shows a lot of interest as I share how we work in an agile manner and the kind of atmosphere we have in my team. I also tell Bernie about Paul's question and what led to it. And that I really don't want to become CEO, because the traditional management style doesn't suit me at all. Besides, I have no clue how I would apply it to the whole organization. Bernie listens carefully until I've finished.

"When I hear you talk, Chris, I think that our way of working at The Facts could really help you and HRS. It is very similar to the way you currently run your department. If you like, I will help you and you can learn more about our approach at the same time."

"Gladly," I answer.

Bernie smiles.

"Great, so I propose that we meet again on Monday afternoon at The Facts offices. Let's say around 1pm? That way you can immediately get a feel for it, which will be much better than me trying to explain it all to you."

"Okay," I say. But I can't hide my disappointment at having to wait until Monday. I'm really curious to find out how Bernie and his colleagues collaborate.

4

THE FACTS

I arrive at the offices of The Facts a bit before one. Bernie serves us both a cup of coffee and takes me along to a cozy corner where we can talk quietly. "We'll be having our monthly governance meeting shortly," Bernie says. "I suggest you join us and observe the meeting. This way you can easily pick up a lot of important and concrete elements of our approach."

"Okay," I say. "But what is a governance meeting?"

"Let's start from the beginning," Bernie says. "We decided to use Sociocracy 3.0 — or S3 , which is the shorthand for it — at The Facts, both to manage our workload and to shape and evolve our processes and our organizational structure. S3 is a recent evolution of the Sociocratic Circle-Organization Method, which was developed in the Netherlands in the seventies. It is a way to govern organizations on the basis of equivalence."

"What makes S3 so powerful," Bernie continues, "is that it combines the sociocratic way of thinking beautifully with the Agile and Lean mindsets."

I look surprised and Bernie laughs.

"Agile?" I ask.

"Indeed. And you know all about it, as I found out on Saturday."

"Hmm, yes," I answer. "We've been using Agile principles in my teams for years. And successfully so. That's why Paul asked me to become the CEO. What a coincidence that these principles are also found in S3!"

"I don't believe in coincidence," Bernie smiles. "Your experience with the Agile philosophy and techniques will help you greatly in applying S3. And I suspect that I will be able to learn a thing or two about the whole Agile approach. I have a background in the Sociocratic Circle-Organization Meth-

> *S3 is a recent evolution of the Sociocratic Circle-Organization Method combined with Agile and Lean principles and techniques.*

od and only became acquainted with Agile when I implemented S3 at The Facts."

Bernie explains that the word sociocracy means 'governed by peers'. It's a form of governance that assumes the equivalence of everyone involved. That is what distinguishes it from autocracy where one person or small group has all the power to make decisions, or from the most typical form of democracy in which decisions are made by, or on behalf of the majority. I'm diligently writing it all down in my notebook. Bernie waits patiently until I've finished before he moves on.

"S3 is a practical guide for enabling more effective and conscious collaboration. The point is to develop more agile and resilient organizations, organizations in which the people working there are engaged and can find fulfillment."

DEFINITION

S3 is a practical guide for conscious and effective collaboration and for creating resilient organizations.

"S3 has several strengths," he continues. "It's available under a creative commons licence, which means it's free to use, and it's modular. Basically, S3 is a collection of mutually reinforcing patterns, and you can choose those that are most helpful to you."

"Patterns?" I ask.

"Yes," Bernie answers. "That's what we call them. If you look at the history of human collaboration, you can see that certain behaviors and practices have emerged and evolved because they help people to work together successfully. Think of patterns as flexible building blocks — you figure out for yourself which are useful in your particular context and put them together in your own way. So S3 is not a top-down, one-size-fits-all method, but rather a backpack filled with great techniques to choose from, which also complement one another."

I'm relieved to hear that. I've come across plenty draconian, all-encompassing methods in the IT world, where you have to change everything at once, according to a specific approach. These methods were often based on good ideas, but usually felt forced and commercially driven.

"And so you choose for yourself which of the patterns to use?" I ask Bernie.

"Right," he continues. "But what I haven't told you is that S3 is based on seven very important principles. These principles create a foundation for the solid implementation of the patterns. And the principles allow for a coherent way of working with S3 in an organization."

"Okay, I understand," I say. "What are the principles, then?"

"A first principle is Equivalence," Bernie explains.

Don't confuse equivalence with equality.

"Ah nice," I interrupt him. "I also treat my people as equals."

"Careful," Bernie reacts. "You shouldn't confuse equivalence with equality, where everyone has to be or do exactly the same. In S3, equivalence means that everyone who is affected by certain decisions should be able to influence these decisions if they have a reason for doing so. This is why many agreements are reached by Consent, which is the second principle. Consent as a principle means we intentionally raise, seek out and resolve objections to decisions and activities. Reasoned objections are welcomed."

"Reasoned objections?" I ask. "What does that mean?"

"Well, we all have opinions and preferences and this can make decision making quite difficult at times. An Objection, however, is an argument that demonstrates or at least helps to reveal why a proposal, or an existing agreement or activity could lead to unintended consequences for the organization. Objections could also include arguments that demonstrate a worthwhile way to improve something."

Consent means raising, inviting
and resolving objections to decisions
and activities.

I nod to show Bernie that I understand what he's saying. At least, I think I do.
"A third principle is Transparency," he continues. "All information and decisions are transparent and accessible to everyone, unless of course there is
a reason for confidentiality, which you can always agree on with consent."
I look up in surprise.
"When you say all information, does that include financial data, such as tar-
gets and salaries? And also strategic decisions?" I ask.
"Yes, in fact, almost everything is transparent in our company," Bernie an-
swers. "With the exception of some details relating to some of our sources,
or other sensitive information."
I'm beginning to understand how the principles reinforce each other, but
Bernie is already moving on.
"Another principle is Accountability. It means that everyone takes initiative
or responds when something is needed and takes ownership for what has
been previously agreed."
"Yes, that's what my software team does as well," I reply enthusiastically.
"They call it commitment. Everyone sticks to what has been agreed upon,
and contributes in a constructive manner, without finger-pointing when
something goes wrong."
"That's exactly what I mean," Bernie confirms. "I'm happy to hear that your
teams are able to do that. It's not to be taken for granted."
"That's true." I say. "And it doesn't always work perfectly. But go on, what are
the remaining three principles?"
"Empiricism is the fifth principle, and it goes together with the sixth one:
Continuous Improvement. Working empirically or in an evidence-based

manner means that you don't continue blindly doing things based on theories or assumptions, but that you learn as quickly as possible from experimentation and concrete results. Knowledge comes from experience and those observations help to continuously learn and improve."

I nod because I know these principles too, from the Agile development approach my teams use.

Decisions have to be good enough for now and safe enough to try.

"An expression we use, is that decisions or solutions have to be 'good enough for now and safe enough to try'," Bernie explains.

"This mainly relates to the principle of consent, but you can clearly see how consent also implies empiricism and continuous improvement. We regularly review and improve agreements we make so they don't need to be perfect, only good enough for now."

"Great," I say. "I can see how these principles all relate to each other. But didn't you say there were seven principles? I noted only six so far."

"Right," Bernie nods. "The last principle is Effectiveness. It refers to focusing on what's necessary to achieve your objectives, removing impediments and eliminating waste."

S3 principles

⭐ Equivalence   ⭐ Empiricism

⭐ Consent   ⭐ Continuous improvement

⭐ Transparency   ⭐ Effectiveness

⭐ Accountability

I'm still writing that last principle down as Bernie moves on.

"So that's the seven principles and they inform all the patterns in S3. They also offer quite a bit of guidance on how to use the patterns in an effective way. But implementing the patterns themselves also helps people to better understand the principles."

"Okay," I say. "Are these principles mandatory, then?"

"No, they aren't. But if you're using S3 patterns, it soon becomes clear why aligning behavior according to these principles can be useful for an organization that wants to better achieve its goals. In fact, you may just come to a point where you want to formally apply the principles in your team or even the organization as a whole. That's why Adopt the seven principles is actually a separate pattern in S3, and it's optional, not mandatory, so people can choose to pull them in if they want to, and in their own way."

"Okay, I think I get the principles. I'd like to learn more about the patterns."

"Before we delve into that," Bernie smiles, "I want to give you a metaphor. I see similarities between an organization and a living organism, such as a city, a tree or a human body. They too are systems that have to constantly adapt to what's happening within and around them. And they don't have a big boss who regulates and dictates everything from above. That wouldn't work, because in a complex system you cannot predict what might happen. Each part reacts to impulses and makes its own decisions in service of the greater whole. That requires a great deal of excellent communication, but it also makes the whole stronger and more flexible."

I nod.

"Looking at it this way," I think out loud, "makes me understand Paul's frustration even more. As HRS is growing, he can no longer respond to all impulses and requests, but his function and our structure expects it of him. Which is slowing us down as an organization."

Bernie nods in agreement.

"Can you tell me more about the patterns?" I ask.

"There are too many to explain them all now," Bernie laughs. "In fact, there are more than 70 patterns defined in S3. But to give you an idea about them: a number of patterns support making decisions in a way that maximally uses the collective intelligence without compromising efficiency. There are also patterns related to participating more effectively in the organization. These are about building motivation and facilitating personal growth. And about increasing accountability, as people intentionally take responsibility for their behavior in service of the organization."

I nod and try to note down as much as possible of what Bernie says.

"There's also a group of patterns that relate to organizing and implementing work," Bernie continues, "to give people more freedom so that they can contribute to the organization in the best possible way. Those are mainly the patterns that come out of Agile and Lean thinking. You probably know them already."

"And the last ones," Bernie says, "are the patterns designed to build an agile and resilient organization."

"Wait a minute," I interrupt Bernie. "What do you mean by building an organization?"

"I mean intentionally defining and evolving the organizational structure according to what's needed," Bernie explains. "For example, S3 has patterns to define roles and circles."

He hesitates, and then continues: "For now, you can consider a Circle to be a semi-autonomous team, although I need to explain its characteristics in more detail later. What's important in the meantime, is that these roles and circles are connected with each other in the right way. That's how, in a bigger organization, you can effectively work together on the same larger goals, and according to the organization's purpose."

Bernie looks at his watch and adds: "The organizational structure clarifies the distribution of work, enables people to be able to influence when necessary, and flows information to the right people in the organization, without having to resort to a power hierarchy."

S3 patterns

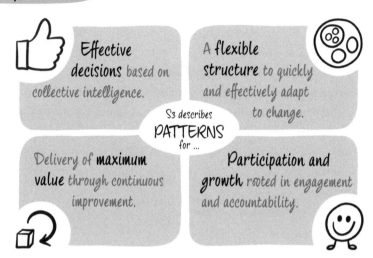

Effective **decisions** based on collective intelligence.

A **flexible structure** to quickly and effectively adapt to change.

S3 describes **PATTERNS** for ...

Delivery of **maximum value** through continuous improvement.

Participation and growth rooted in engagement and accountability.

I nod and want to ask more questions. But Bernie continues: "It's almost time for our governance meeting."

"What does governance mean in this context?" I ask.

"Well, Governance means setting goals and making and evolving decisions that guide people toward achieving them. It typically refers to objectives, processes, agreements and structure in an organization or a team."

"Ah, okay," I say. "So a Governance Meeting is where these types of decisions are made?"

"Yes, that's right. And, in a learning organization, processes, agreements and even roles and teams might be continuously changing or evolving. Which is necessary to be able to accommodate changing contexts, and to respond quickly and effectively to problems and opportunities as they arise. This is a rather different to a traditional organization of course, where structure is typically fixed and rarely changes, except through large and often cumbersome reorganizations."

In a learning organization, processes, agreements and even the organizational structure change constantly.

I nod. I have gone through a few reorganizations in my career, and, in hindsight, without much success.

"But, of course, this doesn't mean that everyone can just go ahead and take whatever decisions they like," Bernie says. "That's why we have these dedicated governance meetings. And this is not the only governance meeting at The Facts. Many of our teams are self-governing and we call these teams circles. Each circle has its own regular governance meetings, where they make decisions about how to effectively account for their area of work."

"What we have today is not an ordinary circle," Bernie explains. "Today, the representatives of five circles at The Facts come together, because these circles need to talk regularly with one another to make decisions on matters that affect them all."

Bernie notices the quizzical look on my face.

"In S3, we typically work with Representatives to link circles with one another," Bernie explains. Teams give their representatives the mandate and the trust to take decisions on their behalf."

"Aha, so you do have some sort of managers," I say.

"No, not at all. These are representatives in the purest sense of the word. They bring the needs, interests and wisdom of their group into the governance meeting of another group. This is called Linking. Taking on the role of representative is temporary; it is not a fixed function. And if we take a decision today and someone in the circle still has an objection to it afterwards, then this decision will be reviewed at the next governance meeting, if not before. Everyone is equivalent here, remember?"

I nod.

"And you do this every month?" I ask incredulously.

"Sure, and some circles have even more frequent governance meetings," Bernie answers. "But let's go now, the meeting starts in a few minutes."

As we walk to the meeting room, Bernie continues to prepare me.

"Obviously you won't understand everything that will happen here, but that's not what's most important," he reassures me. "Just pay attention to how we make decisions together and try to recognize how we apply the seven principles."

"Okay," I say. And though I'm still not very clear on everything, I'm very curious about what is to come.

5

FIRST DOUBTS

"What do you think?" Bernie asks me as we leave the meeting room.

"I don't know what to say," I begin. "It's hard to believe that in barely two hours, you managed to take so many important and sometimes difficult decisions. At HRS, it would have taken several days, if not weeks, to agree on such things, certainly on the decisions about new partnerships or additional salary."

It's hard to believe that in barely two hours, you managed to take so many important and sometimes difficult decisions.

"You're not the first to react like this," Bernie laughs. "But for us, this is the normal way of collaborating and coming to agreements. It's very representative of a typical governance meeting." He pauses for a moment, his eyes sparkling — he is quite obviously proud of their way of collaborating. Then he continues: "Tell me, what else did you notice?"

"Well," I answer. "Perhaps above all, how honest and direct you are with one another. You don't seem to mince words, and I mean that in a positive sense. Everyone is allowed to say what he needs to say or what objections he sees. In our company, we usually bring those up afterwards, in the hallways."

Bernie nods knowingly.

"So, which of the seven principles did you recognize in action during the meeting?"

I think about it for a moment. "Well, the principles of equivalence and consent, for sure. But also accountability. It was beautiful to see how nobody seemed to be afraid to address difficult subjects or to stand up for his idea — without having the need to say stuff that adds nothing to the conversation."

"Right, and that last point of course also has to do with effectiveness. Doing only what helps to advance things. What else did you notice?"

"That you are easily satisfied," I say laughing.

Bernie frowns. "What do you mean?" he asks.

"I don't mean that in a bad sense — on the contrary. You called it: 'Good enough for now and safe enough to try'."

Bernie nods.

"Well, it wasn't until during your meeting that I began to under- *Take a next step in the* stand what this expression really means: You keep taking a next *right direction without* step in the right direction without endlessly looking for an all-en- *endlessly looking for an* compassing solution. For example, when you were developing *all-encompassing solution.* that proposal on the new salaries, you didn't try to cover every single exception. You were looking for a workable solution that you could try for the next few months, and then you'll evaluate, learn and adapt. You win a lot of time that way, I suspect. And on top of that, you develop your approach based on what actually happens, rather than trying to guess everything in advance."

"Indeed," Bernie nods. "I'm happy that you noticed that."

"But now something else," he continues, "because I would like to round up this conversation for today."

He carefully studies me.

"So, Chris, what's your opinion based on what you've experienced today? Do you think it's possible to run HRS more like we do at The Facts?"

"Well, I'm very impressed with what I've seen. Your business is different from ours, but equally complex, it seems to me. So, in theory, it should be possible, yes."

"But?" Bernie smiles, hearing the doubt in my voice.

"I don't know," I sigh. "I still want to think about it a bit."

"Perhaps it would help to first formulate a summary of your driver for becoming CEO and bringing change to HRS," Bernie says.

"My driver! What exactly is that?" I ask. "You all kept talking about drivers in the governance meeting. Does it describe some sort of goal or rationale?"

"Sort of," Bernie nods. "A Driver is an important concept in S3. It's the motive to do or decide something in a specific situation. And in this case, it would be about the reason you would choose to take on the function of CEO, if that's what you want to do. A driver can be summarised by describing two things: what is currently happening and what is needed."

Noticing the confused look on my face, Bernie goes on.

"Let me give a simple example. What was happening on Friday that prompted Kate to call me?"

"I was considering whether to become CEO after all, but didn't think that the way I work on a team level could be applied company wide," I answer.

"Good, that's the first part of the driver, the situation. Now, what did Kate need at that moment?"

"Kate? Well." I feel myself starting to blush. "She told me that she was missing the idealist in me who wanted to change the world and who would go for it. So I think she wanted to help me to feel empowered again."

"Nice, that sounds like the Kate I know," Bernie chuckles. "That's what she needed. And in combination with the situation, this was her driver to give me a call."

I now understand what Bernie means and nod.

"So, clearly understanding the driver to become CEO will help me to make the right decision?" I ask Bernie. "Do I have to write it down?"

"It would probably help," Bernie replies. "If you're clear about a particular situation and about what you think might be needed to respond to it in an effective way, you will often make better decisions."

Before I say goodbye to Bernie, I thank him for allowing me to visit The Facts. The way they collaborated and took decisions together in their governance meeting left a deep impression.

My intuition tells me that I can fully trust Bernie and that I can learn a lot from him. And what I have seen so far about S3 is very promising. So promising, in fact, that I began to question my qualms about accepting Paul's offer to become CEO.

I still don't have the slightest idea how I would begin to change the culture at HRS, or make the company successful again. I don't know whether that's even possible. But I promise myself that tonight I'll do the homework Bernie gave me. Who knows, it might just give me some insight on how to proceed.

6

THE DRIVER

"Phew, definitely more difficult than I'd thought," I say to Kate. She is sitting next to me, watching a TV series while I'm trying to do the homework Bernie gave me.

Kate turns off the TV.

"Tell me why," she says.

"At first, I thought Bernie's assignment was a trick question and that I needed to understand that a CEO is not necessary at all in an organization that relies on self-organization. But that's not true, because I think it is mandatory for HRS as a listed company to have a CEO, at least on paper. I should check. Whatever else, we currently do need a new CEO to help HRS out of its struggle and to lead the company toward becoming a more effective and agile organization."

Kate nods, and I keep thinking aloud. "So, that's the driver that's important for HRS to respond to, but it's not the driver that's motivating me to consider Paul's request to take on the role of CEO."

"Okay," Kate nods. "So what is it that's motivating you then?"

"That's exactly what I'm trying to figure out," I sigh. "I can't put it into words. I'm probably doing something wrong. Or perhaps I shouldn't take on the role of CEO after all."

"Imagine a fairy came to you tonight, waved her magic wand, and took away all your doubts," Kate says smiling. "Who would you put in place as CEO and what would HRS look like then?"

"Oh, you and your difficult coaching questions!" I say, feigning annoyance. But I'm immediately grateful that she wants to help, and we begin to reflect on my driver together.

The conversation with Kate helps me to understand how great it would be if every employee at HRS could do the work he or she loves and does best — without hidden agendas or a cumbersome hierarchy — and energised by their intrinsic motivation.

I begin to imagine all HRS employees organizing themselves in a transparent and effective manner and see a culture emerging at HRS that's completely different from what we have today. I've always been convinced that happy, motivated people tend to make even better products. I see it every day in my own teams. And today at The Facts, I began to realize what this could look like on a larger scale.

Half an hour later, I enthusiastically text a summary of my driver to Bernie. *"HRS has grown a lot and has consequently run into a number of problems: slower decision making, hidden agendas, people who are demotivated, and difficulties in cooperation between departments. I want to fundamentally change the way we collaborate at HRS so that all employees are actively engaged and successfully deliver great products together."*

Bernie fires back immediately: "Very good! I'd be happy to help you to respond to this driver. See you soon!"

"Congratulations," says Kate, who was reading over my shoulders.

"Huh?" I give her a puzzled look.

"Doesn't this mean that you just accepted Paul's offer to become the CEO of HRS?"

I swallow.

"I guess so."

7

THE NEW CEO

It's Wednesday afternoon, and I'm anxiously waiting for Paul to call. He said he would phone me as soon as the board meeting was over.

When I told him this morning that I was ready to take on the role of CEO, he seemed very happy. And despite the drastic changes I had suggested, Paul promised me that he would keep his seat on the board of directors and support me as much as possible. That's when I realized just how impressed he must have been with the way my teams had been working, and the results they had delivered in the previous months. I wondered why he'd never said anything about it before.

Finally, my phone rings.

"Hi Paul, how did it go?" I ask curiously.

"Pretty good, given the circumstances," Paul answers. "Of course there was a lot of anxiety about the missed deadline. That's why I was told today to deliver this version of our product as quickly as possible to reassure our biggest clients and the market, and to regain trust with a follow-up version."

"Sounds logical," I say.

"Yes, but we don't know what the impact would be of delaying the delivery of version 4.0," Paul sighs. "Let's hope many of our biggest clients will still want to buy it, even if it is late. Otherwise that will put even more pressure on the organization."

"And how did they react to your resignation?" I ask.

"Well, I explained why I was resigning and why I believe it's a good time to do so. The reactions were mixed, which isn't surprising, I guess. Nobody thought I was under the degree of pressure that would justify resignation. But they fully understood that real change is necessary and that a new CEO could help with that. At the very least, a new CEO would serve as a signal to clients, to the market — and to the organization itself. So they accepted my resignation, provided that I ensure the current version of our product is delivered as quickly and successfully as possible, which I think is a good idea. It'll allow you to focus on the changes needed in the company and on version 5.0."

"Do you mean…" I barely dare ask the question.

"Yes, congratulations, Chris! You will soon be the new CEO of HRS. The board unanimously approved my proposal to hand the position over to you. And they seemed positive even when I told them about your plans. So it's looking good."

I swallow, happy and tense at the same time.

"Wow, thanks Paul." In the moment, I don't know what else to say.

Paul laughs and reassures me: "I'll help you as much as possible, Chris. Together with the board, I agreed to support you from the sidelines for a few months, to help you with the practical details until you can manage without me. And in any case, along with the project leaders, I'll make sure we deliver version 4.0 as quickly as possible. No change there. This will allow you to grow into your new function at your own pace and to focus on getting the necessary changes in place. I'll remain on the board and of course I'll continue to support you from there. What do you think?"

"That's really great, Paul," I sigh, feeling a load lift from my shoulders. I hadn't been looking forward to having to deal with the problems of the current version.

"This will help tremendously. Thank you so much."

"You're welcome, Chris. I'm personally looking forward to seeing you in action as CEO. HRS really needs the changes that you described during our call this morning. I'm deeply curious about what will happen over the coming months."

8

BERNIE WANTS TO HELP

When I get home from work, Kate and Bernie are waiting for me with broad and welcoming smiles. Kate had secretly invited Bernie to spend the evening with us. I pour myself a glass of wine and flop down on the couch next to Kate. We raise our glasses to my new challenge.

As we walk to the dinner table, I can't resist asking Bernie further questions about how S3 is being used at The Facts. He enthusiastically tells us about temporary but clearly defined roles and circles where people work semi-autonomously to respond to particular organizational drivers. The roles and circles enable them to define their own strategy and organize work themselves.

I learn that rather than choosing a traditional power hierarchy, the organizational structure has evolved over time as people decide how to effectively respond to organizational drivers and distribute the work accordingly. I also learn how all organizational drivers relate in some way directly or indirectly to what they call the primary driver of the organization. And how the overall purpose of the organization is to respond to this primary driver.

Every emerging problem, challenge or opportunity that, if responded to, would help the organization better achieve its objectives, is a meaningful driver. They call these drivers organizational drivers and when anyone becomes aware of such a driver, they either respond themselves, or pass the information on to the right circle or the right role to take it from there. And that is how an organization continuously adapts from within to whatever is needed at any given moment. "Navigating by tension" is what Bernie calls it.

I'm starting to grasp what Bernie said at our first meeting about how this creates an organizational structure that adapts itself to what is needed at any given moment, without requiring fixed functions that hold certain powers.

We have a pleasant evening, and I'm getting an even better picture of how S3 patterns might help HRS. Before he leaves, I ask Bernie whether he was serious when he texted me to say that he would help me to apply S3 patterns at HRS.

"Of course," he says. "Gladly. The business world needs more initiatives like this. I'm happy to contribute."

"Fantastic," I answer with relief. "I really need the help."

"Are you available tomorrow morning?" Bernie asks. "If you are, we could look at some first steps that you can take at HRS."

"With pleasure," I say. "That might be just what I need to prepare for the conversation I'll be having on Friday, when Paul will inform the management team about his decision. He asked me to talk about my plans for HRS in that meeting. So I should make sure I am well prepared."

"Yes, indeed! Then you should start thinking about your approach right away. How do you want to introduce S3 in the organization?"

"Homework again?" I ask and laugh, rolling my eyes.

"Yes," Bernie winks. "See you tomorrow!"

9

INVITATION-BASED CHANGE

I get up extra early. This gives me time to look at Bernie's assignment before I leave for work. Determined to set up the perfect plan, I decide that first there should be clear communication about the upcoming changes. Perhaps I will need to hire a communication specialist.

The following step is a period in which there won't be any changes on the work floor, but together with a handful of people, we will identify all the necessary changes. Which roles and circles need to be established? What will the new agreements and processes look like? Who meets with whom and when? What decisions are to be made, and how? Also, all the drivers will have to be defined so that every role and circle receives clear goals and concrete responsibilities.

Once that is done, everyone will be trained in S3. And only then can we really go about implementing the new way of working throughout the company.

"Are you serious about this?" Bernie asks after I reveal my plan to him in the afternoon. He looks worried.

"Maybe we should start the training sooner?" I cautiously suggest.

"Imagine for a minute that you are one of the HRS employees, someone who doesn't know any of this yet. And then you suddenly get a nice, well-formulated communication about the new CEO and his plans. What is your reaction?"

I fall silent while trying to put myself into that situation.

"I suspect that I would think of it as yet another one of those many changes and joke about it with my colleagues, only to wait and see whether it would really affect me and my work."

"Good," Bernie says. "And suppose that a couple of months later, the plan is ready and being rolled out in the whole company. You have to change your entire behavior and way of working because the CEO said so, and because it is all laid out in a nice document. How would that feel?"

I chuckle.

"Well, I would have an issue with that," I admit.

"And would that make you happier or empower you? Would you want to take more responsibility? Because that's what is spelled out in your driver to become CEO, remember? That is why you are doing all this. The S3 patterns are a tool to accomplish that, no more, no less."

More silence. I don't know what to say and feel crushed. I realize that my beautiful plan won't work at all. On the contrary. How could I have been so stupid?

Luckily, Bernie is not upset. I even notice a twinkle in his eyes.

"This is perhaps the most valuable insight I can give you, Chris," he continues. "Your plan-driven approach may work well enough in some situations, but not for HRS considering where I think it's at right now."

I look questioningly at Bernie, so he explains: "You cannot navigate complexity with a fixed plan. Instead, you want people to be more self-organizing and to allow the right practices to emerge. And you want the company to become more agile as a whole, so that it can readily identify and respond to organizational needs as they arise."

I nod; that is exactly what I want.

"To achieve this," Bernie continues, "you need to evolve a coherent, decentralized approach that frees people to decide and act for themselves where possible, while being assured that they can discuss it with others when necessary or valuable to do so. You want people to be accountable for the consequences of their decisions and to take responsibility for the overall integrity and well-being of the organization as if it were their own."

I nod again. He is right. Imposing a detailed plan from the top on how to achieve all this would set the wrong example.

"But what to do instead?" I ask meekly. I have just lost all my courage.

"Put yourself in the shoes of an HRS employee again. How would you like the new CEO to approach this?"

"I would have to be able to believe in him," I say, as that's the first thing that comes up for me.

"What do you mean by that?"

"Well, if for example he says that we can become more self-organizing and take more decisions on our own, it has to come across as credible and not like some sales pitch."

"Okay, good. And how could he make sure of that?"

I have to think for a while.

"He would have to make clear to me what the advantages would be, not only for the company but also for me personally. I don't think I'd be open to change if I didn't understand the 'why' of it."

Bernie nods.

"And he has to be a role model," I continue cautiously. "For example, I wouldn't want to see him single-handedly taking all the decisions. And I'd appreciate him experimenting with S3 patterns himself. And that applies not only to him, by the way, but to the rest of the management team as well."

"And also," I continue, "it shouldn't end in chaos, with endless discussions where nothing gets decided and nothing gets done."

"Those are already a few important points. It has to be clear why the change is necessary, the CEO and management need to be role models, and whatever you are doing should be helping the organization to create more, not less value," Bernie summarizes. "What else do you need in this scenario?"

"I should be able to choose what I will or won't change, based on what I think is necessary and valuable for the organization."

I look questioningly at Bernie.

"Essentially, yes," he nods. "Enabling and allowing people to choose for themselves how to go about doing work they've taken responsibility for makes sense. That way they develop a strategy that works best for them.

They play to their strengths, take ownership of what they're doing and generally feel more motivated too."

I continue, thinking out loud: "I guess it gets more complicated when there's a group of people who share responsibilities. Because then they need to agree on how to proceed, right? And the principle of consent suggests that we raise, seek out and respond to objections to activities and decisions, right? So, does that mean that anyone, anywhere can raise an objection if they see a reason why something isn't good enough?"

Bernie's eyes say "yes" before he does.

"That's why it would be good to have people's declared intent to fully adopt the principle of consent," he adds.

"Hmm, interesting," I say, and then pause for a moment to reflect.

"I'd probably find information sessions or courses quite interesting, as long as they're not mandatory," I continue. "That way, I can choose which S3 patterns would or would not help me or my team. And perhaps some kind of coach would be a good idea after all, someone with experience who I can ask for help, rather than a manager who will impose things on us."

Change is not only about what's visible in an organization, but also about the invisible: the way people think and their inner patterns.

"Right," Bernie says. "So, non-mandatory trainings and support. And choosing for yourself how you'll go about achieving your objectives."

I nod.

"I completely agree with you, Chris," Bernie states. "I usually call this approach 'Invitation-based change' although I think in S3 the pattern is named Invite Change. In my experience, this is much more powerful than a change that has been worked out in great detail and imposed onto the workforce. Especially in a company such as HRS, which already has a certain level of maturity."

"Invitation-based change, however, doesn't mean that everyone can just do whatever they please," Bernie explains. "As a leader, you first state clear objectives for the organization, and you set the boundaries within which changes and work can be accomplished. Then when you invite your employees to contribute to the necessary changes, they will understand their responsibilities. Their freedom lies primarily in the way they accomplish this, which increases not only their motivation and engagement, but also the quality of the work."

"Change by invitation might initially be slower but you more than make up for this investment later, because it's much more effective in the long run. You not only change what's visible in the organization, such as the structure, the agreements and the behavior, but also the invisible parts, the way of thinking and the inner patterns from which people act."

Bernie stops speaking, and I shuffle uneasily back and forth in my seat. I know that what he says is true but it is so different from what we're used to at HRS.

10

THE MANAGEMENT TEAM

That evening, I tell Kate about the conversation I had with Bernie and about the concept of invitation-based change. The more I talk about it, the more I begin to believe in the idea.

"So, what's your next step?" Kate asks.

"Well, tomorrow I'll meet with Paul and the whole management team. Paul has called the meeting to inform us about his departure and my new function. I think we'll be able to explore some next steps together there too. I'd like to start experimenting with some S3 patterns in the management team as soon as possible, to learn by doing and also to set a good example for the rest of the organization."

"Pretty exciting," says Kate.

"What do you mean?" I ask.

"I'm curious how your direct colleagues will react to the news. You'll suddenly be their boss instead of one of them, won't you?"

"Pfff," I sigh. I hate the word "boss". I've always been happy that in my department I never acted or felt like one. That's precisely why I find S3 so appealing. By putting into place real equivalence, you no longer need a boss or a power hierarchy. By distributing power to influence throughout the organization, people take more responsibility for their areas of work and decision-making.

I'm also aware that not everyone in the management team will think that way. Which is why Kate and I reflect on each manager in turn to discuss what their attitude or reaction could be to me becoming CEO and my idea to try out S3 patterns.

For some, I have no trouble guessing their reactions. I have known Sarah, our ever-cheerful sales and marketing manager, and Carlos, who is respon-

sible for operations and logistics, for years. We get along really well, despite our very different personalities. Sarah loves to learn new things and I suspect she'll happily go along with the experiment. Carlos is much quieter than Sarah, but a hard worker. Like myself, he's a leader who stands with the people, and not above them. That's why I believe he'll be open to my ideas.

I'm certain that Steve will have a harder time with the upcoming changes. He is responsible for all software applications and systems, except the mobile applications which up until now have been my area of responsibility. Although Steve, like me, is only 38, he has always been much more conservative in his approach. He manages his people in a firm and clear manner and monitors nearly every project personally. I understand that his intentions are good and that he wants the best for HRS, but we regularly disagree on things. I hope he's not going to undermine my plans from the start.

How Bart, our data and information manager, will react is more difficult for me to predict. He's quite new at HRS, and I don't know much about his background. I find him a bit reserved, though I've heard people in his team say good things about him.

Julia, our HR manager, will think it's great that I'm going to give people more freedom with S3. She's passionate about motivation and personal development, although her past as a lawyer makes her very strict about rules and regulations. She likes clear agreements. I don't know to what extent our S3 experiments will worry her, but I do expect her to give me a hard time on roles and functions, and perhaps also about evaluations too. When I get a chance I'll ask Bernie what his experiences with these are, because I really want Julia's support for my plan. She can be very convincing to others and that's the kind of support I need.

Then there is Peter, the financial director and also a member of the board. I don't really click with him, but so far that hasn't caused any problems. Given that he's on the board and didn't have objections to my appointment as CEO, I don't expect too much push-back from his side. I make a mental note to check with Paul on how Peter reacted initially.

After my conversation with Kate, I'm a bit anxious about what might await me tomorrow during the meeting with the management team. I wonder whether I should prepare a nice presentation about S3 and my intentions — to appear more sound and convincing.

Casting my doubts aside, I decide not to prepare anything and simply wait for what will happen during the meeting, even if I come across as vulnerable. At least that way I will be honest and true to myself.

11

PAUL'S MESSAGE

"Why Chris?" Steve asks Paul. It's Friday and Paul has just told the management team why he's stepping down as CEO, and that he's asked me to take his place.

"I fully understand your question, Steve," Paul says calmly. "At first sight, Chris seems to be the least logical choice. He's not a typical manager, such as myself or some of you. What's more, he doesn't have any economic or financial background. But Chris is the only one among us who, very naturally, manages to motivate his people and have them work together as a real team. The result: very good software and happy clients. We all know that as well."

Carlos winks at me, and even Steve nods in agreement to Paul's last words. I would have blushed had I not been so nervous.

"And as I just said," Paul continues, "HRS needs a fresh wind to continue to be successful in this market. If we want to differentiate ourselves and continue to make awesome products, we have to become a different kind of company. I can't get that done with my traditional management style. The board and I think that Chris is the perfect person to come up with, and implement, a new and more suitable approach."

Paul pauses and looks around.

"Are there any other questions?" he asks invitingly.

Everyone remains silent, and I take a deep breath of relief. So far so good.

I thank Paul for the trust he places in me.

"Just a few days ago, this was as much of a surprise to me as it must be for you today," I say. "And it feels very strange for me to sit here in front of you. Part of me is scared to death and wants to run away and hide."

Sarah and Julia laugh, and Carlos gives me an encouraging nod. The rest of them also seem curious about what I have to say. So I continue, a bit more reassured.

"Let me get straight to the point. Recently, I have been dreaming about an HRS that is completely self-organizing, without a traditional management hierarchy or slow decision-making processes; moving away from a well-oiled machine where everything has to be predicted and controlled and where people are considered dispensable resources. Because that's what we are in danger of becoming at the moment. I want an organization that functions like a living organism, one that is agile and can respond to external and internal stimuli quickly and effectively. An organization in which people have a lot of freedom while taking a lot of responsibility. Where everyone is empowered to act and where we are all working together toward the overall purpose of the organization."

We want an agile organization in which people have a lot of freedom while taking a lot of responsibility.

I wait a moment to check the reaction of my colleagues. Steve looks at me suspiciously and asks: "And how exactly are you planning to accomplish that, Chris?"

"I'm not quite sure," I answer honestly, looking him straight in the eye. "From my experience with the teams in my department, I know how you can work in a self-organizing way at a team level and how you can organize your work to deliver good products in an agile manner. But I don't yet know how we can use these techniques and principles throughout the organization. The issue is that it's not only a matter of how we organize our work, but also about the way the organization functions as a whole."

I pause.

"I can't do this alone," I say. "I will need your help."

"I think this is very interesting," Julia says. "Count me in."

Steve still looks as skeptical as before, but Sarah, Carlos and even Bart nod in agreement.

Encouraged by their support, I tell them openly about what has happened since Paul first approached me. I explain what I'm learning about S3 and how, at The Facts, using S3 helps them to collaborate in such a smooth and effective way. I tell them about my dream to work like that at HRS as well, but that I need both Bernie and them to find out if it's possible, and how.

Sarah and Carlos are hanging on my every word, and Julia also seems interested. Now and then she asks a brief question, which tells me that she is already trying to imagine what HRS might look like in the future.

I see Bart listening and even taking notes but have trouble guessing what he might be thinking. Peter doesn't provide me with a lot of clues either, although he seems interested and asks some very concrete questions. He wants to know, among other things, how much risk is involved and how quickly we'll see the first results of these changes. These are questions I cannot answer.

I explain that I don't want to impose my ideas and that I want to collaborate with this team and the rest of the organization to discover what concrete changes are needed. I emphasize that I see myself and everyone around the table in a role model function for the organization. And it's my hope that we as the management team can rapidly begin experimenting with S3 principles and techniques. I tell them that it's my intention to avoid imposing anything on anyone, and how doing so would go against the principle of equivalence. Steve interrupts me. "So, if I want I can continue working on my projects as before in my department, without having to change the way I go about doing things?"

I bite my tongue, because I don't believe that Steve's approach to managing his department is the most effective, and he knows that. I've often disagreed with him on how to organize our projects, but I remember Bernie's words about invitation-based change and decide to try to handle the situation delicately.

"Yes, Steve," I say. "I won't use my formal authority as CEO to override you just because we have different opinions about how to go about doing certain things. I intend to focus my attention on working toward achieving what is best for HRS, not on how you or anyone else go about your daily business. I want everyone to make their own decisions as far as possible. You and your people know your work very well and are in the best position to make choices around it. As long as you stay open to feedback from others and make adjustments when there's a good reason for doing so, I'm okay with you getting on with things as you wish."

Steve seems happy with my answer.

"I'd like to start from where we are and see as we go," I continue. "We'll discover which tensions arise, inviting us to reflect and possibly take action. Wherever tensions emerge, change happens spontaneously."

"I'm not sure I understand, Chris," Sarah says looking puzzled.

"Well," I say, thinking out loud. "A tension in this sense is not negative. It's how someone naturally reacts to the dissonance between how they see the current situation and what he or she would expect or wish to see instead. I would like people to respond more consciously to the tensions they experience and to take action themselves if responding to the situation that triggered the tension will contribute to the organization as a whole. For example, by talking to the right people about what is needed."

DEFINITION

Tension is neither negative nor positive. It's a consequence of perceiving a difference between the current situation and what is desired.

"So everyone becomes responsible for the proper functioning of the whole organization," Bart adds. "And would this mean that we won't blame each other as much when things don't go so well, Chris?"

I nod.

"That would be great," Carlos chuckles.

But Julia looks concerned.

"I want to come back for a moment to what you just said about an organization that is constantly in motion," she says. "How does that work with regard to functions and responsibilities? That still needs to be clear and documented. You can't just continuously change our current functions. That's not legally permitted for a company like ours."

"I can't answer that question," I admit honestly. "This is something we'll need to explore together. But of course, whatever we do, we need to stay within the laws and regulations."

My answer seems to satisfy Julia for now. When I finally ask who is willing to begin experimenting with S3, Sarah, Carlos and Julia enthusiastically raise their hands. Bart looks a bit less excited, but he also wants to go along. Steve doesn't respond to my question, just as I had expected. Peter seems doubtful, but finally also says he'll participate.

We decide to start in earnest on Monday, during our weekly meeting with the management team. This gives me the weekend to dive a bit deeper into S3 and to discuss possible first steps with Bernie. And who knows, Steve might still change his mind.

On my way home, I call Bernie and tell him how my colleagues reacted to the news.

"Super," Bernie says. "And what are your next moves?"

"We agreed that this coming Monday, we'll take our first steps and start experimenting with S3," I explain.

"Seems like a good idea to me," Bernie says. "How can I help you with this?"

"Well, firstly I'd like to understand S3 a bit better," I answer. "Particularly regarding governance meetings and how decisions are taken there. And how we define roles within our team. I don't know enough about that yet. Do you have a bit of time to explain that to me before I meet the team on Monday?"

"Yes, sure," Bernie replies. "But perhaps I have an even better idea. Would you like me to join your meeting on Monday? I'm very curious about your organization and your colleagues. And then I can explain S3 to all of you a bit more and help you with the first steps."

"Oh, that would be fantastic, Bernie," I answer.

I'm really happy with Bernie's support, and I'm already looking forward to the meeting with him and my colleagues on Monday.

12

DRIVERS AND DOMAINS

After I've introduced Bernie and the management team to one another on Monday morning, Bernie immediately takes the lead.

"Hello everybody," he says with a friendly smile. "Chris invited me to this meeting to explain S3 to you in a very practical way. Not to give you theoretical training on it, but to apply S3 as we go through the items on your agenda today. This way we can learn by doing."

"Both S3 and I are new to you," Bernie continues. "I understand that all too well. This is why I would first like to ask you whether anyone has an objection or concern about me being here and proceeding in this way."

"No, not at all," Sarah responds with a big smile. There are no apparent objections from the others either.

"Fine," Bernie says. "Then I would like to immediately introduce an S3 pattern called Check in to get us started. Are you familiar with this?"

Nobody knows what Bernie means, so he explains: "It helps a great deal to be mentally and physically present in a meeting like this. And at work in general too," he adds as an afterthought. "So, before getting started, we all take a turn to briefly share what's going on with us at the moment. I mean in life in general, not just with work. By doing so, you'll find it's easier to put aside thoughts or feelings that could otherwise distract you. It's also a chance for your colleagues to learn something about what's alive in you, and they'll consciously, or subconsciously at least, take this into account throughout the day. Showing your vulnerability to one another also increases trust between you and so will help improve collaboration."

"So we just say how we are, one by one?" Bart asks. He looks quite skeptical. "Will this not turn into a sort of coffee klatch?"

"No, that's not the purpose, Bart," Bernie answers, smiling in acknowledgment. "A report on how the weekend went is indeed something for later at the coffee machine. During a check in, everyone who wants to — because it is not mandatory — briefly shares what has their attention at the moment, what they need to name to be able to be more present. This could include how you are feeling, what's on your mind or something that's distracting you. You might want to ask something of the group that would help you to be more present and focused in this meeting."

"One by one," Bernie continues, "we share a few words or sentences, preferably no more than that. And the others listen attentively. There's no need to jump in or help with anything, it's just about being present and giving each other the space to land."

DEFINITIE

A check in gives everyone the opportunity to express what's alive in them, helping them to be more present and focused.

I look around curiously. I'm familiar with this type of language from the meditation group that I was part of for a few years. But I'm aware that not everyone around this table is into those things.

Bernie sets the example and starts the check in: "I feel fully present and I'm excited to introduce these techniques to a company such as yours. And I'm curious to discover whether and how I'll be able to support you in this journey."

Before continuing, Bernie introduces the Rounds pattern. We will go around the circle as we are seated, sharing in sequence, so everyone gets a chance to speak and it's always clear who goes next. As I'm sitting next to Bernie, I share my enthusiasm about this meeting and the fact that I'm also nervous about not knowing where this will all end. The rest of the group follows one by one, hesitantly, but we manage to remain brief and to not interrupt one another. Only Steve passes and skips his turn.

There is a noticeable change in the atmosphere after the check in. It's calmer somehow. I promise myself to do this more often at the beginning of a meeting.

———

"Tell us, Bernie," Sarah says. "What is the best way to begin with S3? Which parts of it do we implement first?"

She is impatient, as she so often is when she is enthusiastic about something.

Bernie smiles. "Let's start at the beginning," he says.

We listen carefully while Bernie shares a bit more about The Facts and explains the purpose and the background of S3. Next, he guides us through the seven S3 principles and names some of the most important patterns. Bernie is a good storyteller, and everyone is hanging on his every word. Even Steve seems somewhat interested. Peter and Bart are busy taking notes.

"Let me come back to your question, Sarah," Bernie says, concluding his introduction. "What would be the best way to begin using S3? Well, as you've been learning just now, it's not that you use all the patterns at the same time. That doesn't make any sense at all. Rather it's about experimenting with one or even a few patterns that would add value at the moment, based on what's actually happening and needed in the organization. And to be very clear with you, I don't think it is a good idea to just go ahead and impose S3 patterns on a team or an organization."

"Mmm," Sarah thinks aloud. "What do you mean? Shouldn't we as the management team be telling people what to do?"

"Great question," Bernie acknowledges. "You as the management team definitely need to ensure that certain matters are dealt with effectively throughout the organization. And I'm confident that S3 will help you with that. But in my opinion it's more effective to highlight what the needs are and then support people in effectively responding to them, than it is to impose a particular approach and expect them to follow blindly. You should invite them to make such a decision for themselves."

Don't start with all S3 patterns at the same time. Experiment with one or a few patterns that would add value at this moment.

He winks at me and continues: "So, let's not make an extensive multi-year plan but just have a look at what is needed. This way we will learn by doing whether and how S3 can support you. Okay?"

Everyone nods.

"Good," Bernie continues. "Tell me, what important things are going on at the moment at HRS or in your team? And what is it that's needed?" I notice that he is looking for drivers, and I deliberately wait to see what the others come up with before I answer his question.

"Well," Carlos responds. "I think that the news that Chris has become CEO is the most important thing. As well as the need to communicate to all employees about it." He looks around, and most of us nod.

"Yes," Peter adds. "And with regard to communication, we need to assign a new spokesperson. Paul will no longer take on that role, and the press will show up at our doorstep as soon as the news about his resignation spreads." Again, everyone nods. Except Julia; she seems to have doubts.

"Julia?" I ask.

"Don't get me wrong," she begins cautiously. "I agree with you that the spokesperson and communication are an urgent matter. But isn't the reason for Paul's resignation a more important subject? HRS is not doing well, and changes are necessary to stay healthy as a company."

"This is definitely really important," Carlos agrees.

"What would you think if for now we started with these three items," Bernie chimes in. "No doubt we could come up with many more topics, but I think these are a few urgent and important items that we could tackle. Does anyone have an objection to this?"

No one seems to object to his proposal. I notice that Steve is keeping to the side, avoiding eye contact. He probably doesn't like any of this, but wants to wait and see. I decide to say nothing for now.

Bernie continues: "One first and very important concept in S3 are drivers. A driver is a person or a group's motive for responding to a specific situation.

Everything begins with a driver, whether we are talking about setting up and running a whole organization or the daily decisions made by a team or individual."

A driver is a person or a group's motive for responding to a specific situation.

"That's why you asked us what important things we should be working on?" Sarah inquires.

"Exactly," Bernie replies. "I was looking for a few important drivers that are currently alive in your team."

"It's helpful to Describe Organizational Drivers," he continues. "You summarize a driver clearly, including a description of what's happening. This is the current situation as it is perceived objectively and the actual or anticipated effect it has on the organization. A good driver summary also outlines what is needed by briefly summarizing the organization's need in relation to this situation and what the expected impact would be if this need was attended to. By describing all of these aspects clearly, the context of the need is framed and can be understood."

Describing drivers

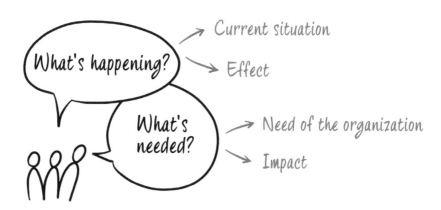

"Let's give it a try?" Bernie suggests. "That will make it clear. Shall we begin with the driver you mentioned, Julia? About the change that is needed at HRS?"

It takes a while before we all agree on the description of the driver. Bernie helps us patiently and writes our final result on the flip chart. *"Due to the current structure and culture at HRS, we're confronted by a number of problems such as demotivation, slow decision making and ineffective collaboration between teams. This has prevented us from launching version 4.0 successfully, and puts HRS at risk. We need to become more agile and effective as an organization, so that we can create and deliver awesome products again in the near future."*

Silence reigns as we all look at the driver. It's as if the gravity of the situation is only now sinking in for everyone.

Bernie finally breaks the silence. "As you can see from this exercise, summarizing a driver helps to create shared understanding of what exactly is happening and what is needed. And subsequently, to decide on actions to deal with the situation and work toward achieving your desired goals."

We nod.

"It also makes very clear why we are going to do something, or want to change something," Sarah comments. "We should do this more often, shouldn't we? Clarifying our drivers, I mean."

She looks around the table. It's true, we often take action without first agreeing on why we are doing it or how important something is.

"Actually, you could also see describing an organizational driver together as a form of Agreement," Bernie says. "You agreed as best you could on what is actually happening, and what you think is needed, which creates a common focus."

"And given that this is an agreement or decision that you made together," Bernie continues, "it would be good to decide at what point in time you'll re-evaluate this agreement."

> *Every agreement gets a review date to regularly check on its effectiveness.*

"What do you mean?" Carlos asks.

"Well," Bernie explains, "S3 has a pattern called Evaluate and Evolve Agreements. It's a way to put into practice the principles of empiricism and continuous improvement, as well as the principle of effectiveness. In other words, checking that you're focusing efforts on doing what needs to be done to achieve your objectives. S3 invites you to set review dates and the frequency of these for every significant agreement you make. That way, we commit to checking on a regular basis whether decisions we took earlier are still relevant and effective. This includes considering the driver behind an agreement itself because a situation may change over time, requiring adjustments to how a driver is summarized. Or it may be that a driver has been responded to in the meantime."

"This also relates to what I mentioned last week about becoming more self-organizing," I add. "If we want HRS to become agile so that we can quickly and effectively respond to the needs of our clients and the market, our internal processes, work agreements and structure also need to adapt continuously. Setting a review date is one of the mechanisms to build in continuous evaluation and improvement."

"Right," Bernie says. "This doesn't mean that you have to wait until the review date of an agreement to be able to change things if necessary. On the contrary, if we discover tomorrow that this agreement is no longer good enough, we can respond immediately and adapt it."

"Super," Sarah says. "Shall we then set a review date for this agreement and go on with our other two drivers?"

"Unless someone still has a question," I respond. While I'm happy with her enthusiasm, I want to be sure that everyone understands the S3 narrative. I think it is really important that we fully grasp these principles.

Bernie helps us with decently summarizing the other two drivers. It's beginning to go much more smoothly, and before long, these drivers are also neatly written on the flip chart.

"As a next step, let's have a look at how we can respond to these three drivers," Bernie suggests. He reads one of the drivers: *Paul resigns as CEO, and Chris takes on that role. This needs to be communicated to all employees quickly and clearly to avoid unnecessary confusion.*"

"What's needed to respond to this driver?" Bernie asks us.

"Well, I don't know whether it's a coincidence," Peter says, "but we'd planned an all-hands meeting for next Friday. Would that not be a good moment?"

Bernie raises his eyebrows and looks at me questioningly.

"The all-hands meeting is a short monthly meeting with the whole company," I explain. "It's during this meeting that Paul typically talks about the state of affairs and shares any news with the employees."

Bernie nods. We quickly agree that giving a transparent and clear explanation at this gathering seems to be the best solution. This way, everyone gets to hear the same story. I take it upon myself to discuss this with Paul and to prepare the content of this communication before next Friday.

"So," Bernie concludes our conversation. "Will Chris's action sufficiently respond to this driver?"

"Yes, good enough for now and safe enough to try," Sarah chuckles.

She is referring to the explanation Bernie gave earlier on the S3 principles. The rest of the group nods as well.

"Perfect," Bernie says. "Because I want to tell you more about responding to drivers. Let's do so by using the next driver we summarized: *In addition to being CEO, Paul was also the spokesperson, and he will give up that role as well.*

We need a new spokesperson who will take over those tasks and communication to ensure that HRS is well represented in the media."

"I think we should create or describe a domain for this driver," Bernie explains. "A Domain is a distinct area of influence, activity and decision-making within an organization. You can also look at it as the area in which responsibility has to be taken to respond to a driver."

> **DEFINITION**
>
> *A domain is a distinct area of influence, activity and decision-making within an organization.*

On a new sheet, Bernie draws a circle with the letter "D" in the center. He explains that the "D" represents the driver and that the circle represents the domain. He goes on to explain that a domain is a recognizable and clearly delimited area of work within an organization, in which activities and decisions are needed to respond to the driver.

When he sees that we understand, he writes "Domain Description" on top of the sheet.

"It often makes sense to Clarify Domains, meaning making them explicit by describing them," he explains. "This way, you ensure that everyone shares the same understanding. The first part of a domain description is the driver. In our case, we already have that. We call it the primary driver of the domain."

He points again to the circle in which the "D" represents the primary driver of this domain.

Bernie begins to list the elements of a useful domain description. He writes "Primary Driver" on the page, and below he copies the driver in question. When that is done, he adds "Delegator: Management Team" as a second element.

"You are the ones that hold overall accountability for this driver and the domain we're creating," Bernie explains. "That makes you the so called 'delegator' for this domain. You are delegating the responsibility to respond to this driver to the spokesperson, together with the autonomy to do so within this domain's boundaries."

We nod, to show we understand. Bernie goes on and adds "Key Responsibilities" as the third element of the domain description.

"Often, a few important responsibilities are added to the domain description," he states. "Another way of looking at these responsibilities is to think of them as essential subdrivers that should be responded to, to effectively account for the domain."

Bernie gives us a bit of time to let his words sink in.

"So, the ones we will list here are the most important, but not necessarily all the subdrivers?" Bart asks.

Bernie nods. "Exactly! They include key deliverables relating specifically to the primary driver, as well as drivers relating to the organizational context."

"How many are there?" Sarah asks. "For some domains you could easily come up with hundreds of subdrivers."

You don't make up or invent drivers; you simply summarize what is actually happening and what is needed.

"Don't forget that there is no need to make up or invent a driver." Bernie reminds us. "You summarize what is happening in reality and what is needed. And this is also true for this list of subdrivers. Often it's enough to name and write down between three and seven key responsibilities, meaning only the most important ones. Although in some cases you may decide it's helpful to describe more."

"Okay," Sarah nods.

"If we apply this to our spokesperson domain," Bernie continues, "which key responsibilities do you see there?"

"To properly handle formal economic and financial communication," Peter says spontaneously. "That's really important for a listed company."

"Okay," Bernie says as he writes it down on the flip chart below the driver. "Anything else?"

"What about to control all stock market sensitive communication?" Julia asks. "We sometimes have to be very cautious and mindful in our communication about our products — for instance, being late with version 4.0."

Peter nods.

"And in our less formal communication, such as for interviews or on social media," Sarah adds. "Did Paul handle those things too?"

"No," Peter says, "but he did keep an eye on it and was ready to help where needed."

We decide that these are the most important responsibilities and add them to our list on the flip chart.

Another element of a domain description details any preferred qualities, skills and experience needed to effectively account for the domain. Bernie helps us to sum up the most important expectations in this regard and encourages us to stick to the essence to keep the domain description lightweight and clear.

"Are there certain restrictions or constraints to this domain that are important?" Bernie asks further. "Such as limited budget or time? Or certain agreements that need to be respected in your work?"

We look at one another with some hesitation.

"Well," Peter says. "There are some kinds of legal constraints within which we may communicate as a listed company, related to stock market sensitive information and dealing with insider knowledge and such."

We nod, and Bernie records this in our domain description.

"Are there any other constraints or limitations in this regard? Maybe dependencies, or a specific kind of reporting that's required."

"Hmm," Sarah says. She hesitates. "I don't know whether this is a constraint, because it often helped Paul more than it hindered him."

"Tell us," Bernie encourages her.

"Well," Sarah explains. "Paul and I had some kind of implicit agreement that he would briefly check most communication with the marketing team first. We helped him with copywriting for written communication, or took care of the proper branding or positioning of our product in his story."

"Cool," Carlos reacted, "I didn't even know that."

"This is a nice example of when a constraint on a domain can be both limiting and enabling," Bernie responds. "And that's why a good domain description also includes details of the most important resources that are available to support responding to the domain's primary driver. These could be budget and time, but also tools or any other type of support. Let's include the support of the marketing team as a resource on the spokesperson's domain description."

After adding it to the flip chart, Bernie asks: "Can you see how this domain description, with key responsibilities and constraints, clarifies the area of autonomy for whoever takes it on?"

A domain description clarifies the area of autonomy and responsibility.

I nod. I can clearly see how it helps to explicitly define a domain. "Not really," Sarah says apologetically. "I'm still not entirely clear on what exactly a domain is."

"I'm happy to hear that," Bernie reassures her. "Would one of you like to explain it to Sarah in your own words? It'll be a good way for me to check how what I told you has come across."

"I want to give it a try," Bart says. "Do you understand what a driver is?" he asks Sarah.

"Yes, I think so," she says. "A driver is the reason for responding to a situation. And we become aware of them by considering why we are experiencing tension in certain situations and understanding what's happening and what we think is needed."

"Right," says Bart. "And as I understand it, the domain you create for a driver is that part of an organization in which decisions and actions are taken to respond to that driver. To put it differently, the area in which people are given autonomy to take the necessary decisions and do the work needed to take care of the driver."

Bernie nods.

"Ah, right." Sarah says giving Bart a big smile. "It's clearer now."

"Thank you, Bart," Bernie says. "So we're almost done with our domain description. All we need to do now is to add review frequency and Evaluation Criteria. This will tell us when and what we'll evaluate to learn how effectively this domain is being accounted for and its driver responded to. In a minute, I'll explain more about how people organize themselves in a role or a team to take responsibility for a domain. But first it helps to understand that with S3 it's customary to look for regular feedback — both as an individual and as a team — on what works well and what could be even better. That's how you arrive at an improvement or development plan. This pattern is called Peer Review, and I'll explain in more detail when the time comes."

"Interesting," Julia says.

I'm also curious about peer reviews. But that'll have to wait a while because before we can ask more questions, Bernie brings us back to our domain description. We decide to set the review frequency at three months and therefore to schedule a peer review every three months. Next, Bernie helps us to formulate a few criteria that we can use to help us with the evaluation.

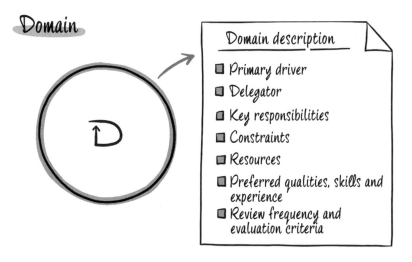

Our first domain description is born! We have the driver, the key responsibilities, the preferred qualities, skills and experience, constraints, resources and some evaluation criteria and a review frequency nicely summarized on the flip chart. Bernie rewards us with a break.

"And, what do you think?" I ask the others as we walk to the cafeteria for a cup of coffee.

"Super," Sarah beams. "I think that summarizing drivers will really help us."

"Exactly," Carlos chimes in. "At least now we'll know why we do the things we do, and we can choose more consciously what we want to focus on."

"I'm especially curious about what's still to come," Julia says. She looks at Bernie. "I suppose you will also teach us about the other ways of responding to a driver, won't you?"

Bernie nods.

"Nice," Julia responds. "I'm interested in the link with our teams and departments."

Bernie wants to answer, but Sarah interrupts him as we arrive at the cafeteria: "A cup of coffee, Bernie?"

"Yes, thank you," he replies. "Black, please."

While we take our drinks and sit down, Bart asks Bernie how many patterns S3 describes. Bernie doesn't know offhand but guesses that there are about 75.

"Oh no!" Sarah exclaims. She'd knocked over a cup of coffee.

"No problem," I say. "I'll get a cloth."

"Wait a minute, Chris," Carlos says. "Let's summarize the driver first before you jump into action. What's happening and what's needed?"

We all laugh at his joke. All except Sarah, who is preoccupied with trying to prevent the coffee from spilling onto her dress. I quickly get a cloth.

When I join them again, Bernie is busy talking about The Facts. I listen with only half an ear and look around the table. Sarah and Carlos seem completely relaxed, hanging on his every word. Bart and Julia are talking about something else and Peter is looking at emails on his cell phone.

"Where is Steve?" I ask Peter.

"Oh, he just left," he replies. "Probably to the toilet."

"Really?" I ask. "I thought he went just a minute ago."

Peter shrugs and goes back to his emails. I decide not to think about it anymore and listen to the stories about The Facts until it's time to get back to work.

13

ROLES, CIRCLES AND STEVE

Steve is already in the meeting room when we arrive.

"Technical problem," he says apologetically as he closes his laptop. "I had to make sure that my people can at least continue."

"Shall we go on?" Bernie asks. "We were talking about drivers and their domains. Now I want to explain the different ways in which people Respond to Organizational Drivers, thereby creating and evolving an organizational structure that is constantly adjusted to suit their context."

Everyone appears eager for Bernie to go on. He seems to have quickly gained the trust of my colleagues, all except Steve, whose thoughts seem to be elsewhere. I'm sure Bernie notices it too but he doesn't seem bothered by it.

"The most common way to respond to a driver," Bernie explains, "is with some kind of direct action or with an agreement. Agreements include the decision to clarify a domain and to delegate responsibility for it to an individual in a role or to a group of people in some kind of a team."

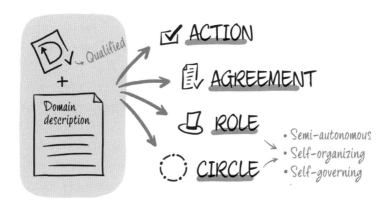

He looks around the table to check whether everyone is following him and continues: "We just saw an example of direct action in that Chris will take care of the communication in the all-hands meeting, which responds adequately to the driver. But often, a one-off action is not enough to effectively respond to a driver."

"As in the case with our spokesperson," says Julia.

"Exactly," Bernie agrees. "Here it seems that a Role would be the most appropriate pattern to use. S3 has a related pattern called Role Selection, which you can use to choose someone to take responsibility for a role.

> **DEFINITION**
>
> *A role is a domain's area of responsibility which is delegated to one person.*

"The person taking on a role," Bernie continues, "is called the role keeper. And he has the freedom to take decisions and to organize the work within the constraints of the role's domain."

"Ah," responds Julia. "Now I begin to understand the value of clearly clarifying domains in practice. In this case, it defines the purpose of the role and sets any necessary constraints."

"Correct," says Bernie. "When creating a role, the domain description becomes the role description. We call it a role domain description. The only additional detail we should add to a role domain description is the term for which someone can hold that role. When a person's term comes to an end, the role selection process is repeated and a new person is selected. Of course, the same person could be selected again, depending on the circumstances."

"What's the difference between a role and a function?" Julia interrupts.

"Good question," Bernie says. "The biggest difference is that appointment to a role is always temporary and sometimes even for a short time. The decision to account for a domain with a role, and on who is selected, are all agreements made by the group who created it, and so they are re-evaluated at regular intervals. This helps to check whether a role adequately responds to a driver or whether it needs to be adapted. Or if the choice to account for the domain with a role was the right one at all. Further, sometimes a driver is adequately responded to and the role becomes redundant. Or, in the meantime, more people are required to work on that driver and so a team is chosen instead."

"Moreover, people can take on several roles at the same time," Bernie goes on, "which is usually not the case for functions."

Julia nods. "And I assume that a role is not linked to a specific salary, is it?" she asks.

"You're right," Bernie says. "Usually, it isn't."

"Hmm," Julia thinks out loud. "Then we have to learn how to work with both our new roles as well as with our existing functions, because we can't just get rid of our current functions. This would create issues with our employment contracts and HR legislation."

"True," Bernie nods. "How about we discover as we go which drivers arise around this topic and find solutions based on what's possible in the moment."

"That's fine," says Julia, smiling broadly at Bernie.

I'm glad they get along so well.

"Can I jump back to what you just said about regularly re-evaluating agreements, Bernie?" Bart asks. "That sounded important but I didn't entirely get it."

"Of course," Bernie responds. "I was referring to a very important pattern in S3 called evaluate and evolve agreements. It's a way to put the principles of empiricism and continuous improvement into practice, as well as the principle of effectiveness. To evaluate and evolve agreements means that every significant agreement you make gets a review date and frequency. That way, we regularly check whether decisions we took earlier are still relevant and effective. This includes considering the driver behind an agreement itself because a situation may change over time, requiring adjustments to how a driver is summarized. Or it may be that a driver has been responded to in the meantime."

"This also relates to what I mentioned last week about becoming more self-organizing," I add. "If we want HRS to become agile so that we can quickly and effectively respond to the needs of our clients and the market, our internal processes, work agreements and structure also need to adapt continuously. Setting a review date is one of the mechanisms to build in continuous evaluation and improvement."

"Right," Bernie says. "This doesn't mean that you have to wait until the review date of an agreement to be able to change things if needed. On the contrary, if we discover tomorrow that this agreement is no longer good enough, we can respond immediately and adapt it."

"Wait a minute," Bart interrupts him as he looks through his notes. "When we created the domain description for the spokesperson, we added a review frequency and evaluation criteria, indicating when a peer review should happen. Correct?"

"Yes," Bernie confirms.

"And now we learn that every agreement should get a review date, to check and improve the agreement itself," Bart goes on. "But that's not what is happening in a peer review, is it?

"Great question, Bart," Bernie smiles. "What do you think the difference is?"

Bart checks his notes again, and then says: "I think evaluating and evolving agreements is about regularly reviewing and, if needed, improving the decision or agreement itself. Which applies to any kind of decision or agreement. While a peer review is about evaluating people."

"Yes, exactly," Bernie says, "although I don't like to use the term 'evaluating people'. It sounds so unfriendly. What is being evaluated is how effectively they've been in accounting for a certain domain and how well they've been responding to its primary driver."

Bart nods and I notice the others also appear to understand it better now.

"Okay," Bernie says. "Where were we before we got into all these interesting questions?"

"You had explained how a role is one way to account for a domain," I answer.
"Right," Bernie nods. "If you don't need one single person but a multidisci-
plinary team to take responsibility for a domain, a common practice in S3 is
to create a circle. A circle is a special type of team with distinct properties.
There are some other, less common, team patterns in S3 too but I'll clarify
those when the time comes."

"A circle's domain is clarified in the same way as for a role," Bernie continues. "The members of a circle are equivalent and work semi-autonomously.
This means they organize their work themselves, within the constraints of
their domain."

DEFINITION

*A circle is a self-governing and semi-autonomous
group of equivalent people who collaborate to
take responsibility for a domain.*

"A circle is also self-governing within the constraints of its domain. This is
why the members of a circle regularly hold so-called governance meetings.
Governance is about setting objectives, and making and evolving decisions
that guide people towards achieving them. For instance, setting constraints
within which the required work is to be done."

"And how often should they have such governance meetings?" Peter asks.
"Do they invest a lot of time in them?"

"Well, that depends," says Bernie. "As much time as necessary, but no more
than that. Some teams hold bi-weekly meetings, others only once a month.
And it's not as if all governance decisions are made in a scheduled meeting. Sometimes circle members conduct governance on the go, during the
course of their daily work."

Peter seems reassured by his answer. Bernie looks around the table for a moment to check whether everyone else is following along. Apparently everyone is.

"So, to summarize," he continues, "drivers can be responded to by creating a domain and then accounting for it with a role or a team. And remember, a circle is a specific kind of team. You can also respond to a driver by making any other kind of agreement, such as working agreements for example. Such an agreement usually applies to the domain within which it was established. These types of agreements get an evaluation date and evaluation criteria, and are regularly reviewed and, if needed, adapted, just like roles and circles."

"In fact, roles and circles are also some kind of agreement that you make, aren't they?" Bart asks.

"Right, Bart," Bernie answers. "Another clever observation."

"So that means that the decision to respond to a driver by creating a domain and accounting for it with a role also needs to be evaluated on a regular basis," Bart thinks aloud. "Doesn't that mean that you have an awful lot of evaluations in these governance meetings?"

"Yes and no," Bernie explains. "It's true that it is good to check in every governance meeting whether agreements have to be evaluated. But that doesn't always need to take a lot of time. And it is often done by combining a number of items, such as the evaluation of a driver, the domain description that goes with it and whether to respond to it with a role or a circle. In this case you treat it as one agreement that is being evaluated."

Bart nods. It's clear to him. I'm happy with his questions. It shows me that he's reflecting on what Bernie is saying.

"Does that mean that you have to set up an action, an agreement, a role or a circle for every driver?" Peter asks. "Or even define every single driver?"

"No, not at all," Bernie reassures him. "It's impossible to explicitly describe every driver and nor would you want to. After all, if you think about it, there's a driver underlying every intentional decision or action you take. Summarizing a driver becomes helpful when you discover an organizational need or opportunity that is not effectively responded to spontaneously. Or when you want to communicate about a driver to someone *After all, there's a* else, or when people seem to have different points of view about *driver underlying every* a situation." *intentional decision or action you take.*

Peter nods. He seems satisfied.

"May I ask you something else about domains?" Sarah says, frowning.

"Of course," Bernie smiles.

"Given that there are a lot of drivers within an organization, there will also be several domains, right? How are they all connected?"

Bernie is clearly happy with this question. He gets up to draw on the flip chart as he answers it.

"As Sarah pointed out, there are several drivers existing in an organization at any time. It begins with the primary driver, in other words the reason an organization exists and was created to begin with."

Bernie draws a big "D" in the middle of the sheet to represent the primary driver, with a number of smaller subdrivers around it.

"Every new driver that arises within the organization," he continues, "should be qualified. This means that we verify whether or not responding to this driver would help the organization generate value, eliminate waste or avoid undesired consequences. If it does, we call it an organizational driver."

DEFINITION

A driver is considered an organizational driver if responding to it would help the organization generate value, eliminate waste, or avoid unintended consequences.

Bernie connects the subdrivers he has drawn with the primary driver so it looks like a mindmap.

"It's a network of interrelated drivers," he explains. "And as you learned earlier this morning, a domain can be explicitly created around any driver when it makes sense to define one."

Bernie draws a circle around every driver to illustrate domains.

"Some domains also share dependencies too," he continues, drawing another D between two of the domains and then adding another circle that embraces that D and overlaps both of the domains. The result is a large circle around the primary driver, and a number of smaller circles around the subdrivers with overlapping domains.

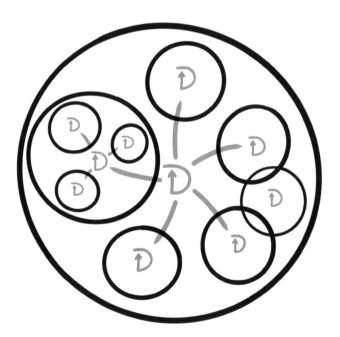

"As I said earlier, a domain is a distinct area of influence, activity and decision making required to respond to a driver," he continues. As you can see, an organization consists of a number of nested domains and some can overlap as well."

"A heterarchy instead of a hierarchy," Bart nods.

"A what?" Carlos asks. The looks of the others show that Carlos and I are not the only ones who have never heard of a heterarchy.

"In a heterarchy, the various elements are not arranged on a higher or lower level in relation to one another, but are equivalent," Bart explains. "A heterarchy puts the focus on self-organization and decentralized decision making. The structure is emergent and configured according to the needs of the system at any given moment. This might include hierarchies but some areas can be flat or bottom-up as well."

"Exactly," Bernie says. "In S3, the elements Bart talks about are called domains. In the context of an organization, they can also be seen as the roles and teams that account for those domains, defining the structure of an organization."

"Please understand," Bernie adds with a grin, "this drawing is an extreme simplification of reality. In real life, domains can interrelate and overlap in many different ways. Sometimes an organizational map can look more like a multidimensional plate of spaghetti than a pan full of eggs, but you get the idea!"

The organization continuously adapts itself to what is needed to maximally respond to its primary driver.

Everyone smiles.

"Now I'm beginning to understand what an entire organization could look like from the point of view of S3," says Julia. "Cool."

"And that's how the structure continuously changes then, as domains are created, reviewed and evolved according to what's needed," Carlos adds.

"Right," I say. "Because new drivers are always emerging in an organization. They have to be dealt with through actions and agreements, including creating new roles and teams. This allows an organization to adapt to whatever is needed at any given moment to maximally respond to its primary driver. Just like in any living system."

"And that," Bernie says gravely, "is perhaps one of the most important S3 patterns to help you become an agile organization. It is called Navigate Via Tension."

"Oh, tensions," says Sarah. "That's what Chris was talking about earlier. And how by understanding what triggered tension in us, we discover new drivers."

"Exactly," Bernie answers. "If we're navigating via tension then a driver must first be qualified, which means checking if it's relevant for the organization to respond. Assuming it is, then the driver is passed on to the domain it belongs in within the organization. The people responsible for that domain take the necessary decisions and carry out the work required to respond to the driver. Which can include making changes to the organization itself, such as adapting existing domains or creating new ones and deciding how to account for them."

Navigate via tension

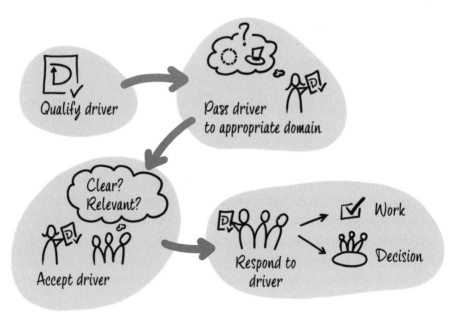

"That's how an organization navigates through the complex world it lives in," I add.

Silence reigns in the group. Peter doesn't seem entirely at ease, and Carlos is frowning as he looks at the drawing. I notice that this meeting is beginning to have an impact, which is good, I think.

"No worries, dear colleagues," I reassure them. "We'll tackle this step by step. I suggest that as a first step we experiment with S3 patterns in the management team to learn for ourselves and set a good example. Those who see an opportunity and have the energy can begin right away with small experiments in their own departments too, which is how this will grow step by step. We'll invite the organization and the teams to change, but without imposing anything. Individuals and teams can choose for themselves what they will or will not do, okay?"

Everyone nods. Except Steve.

"You're not going to impose anything on us or our departments?" he asks.

"That's right," I answer.

"Then I won't be part of it," he says resolutely. "And neither will my department."

The room is so quiet, you could hear a pin drop. Everyone looks at me, and I have no idea how to react.

"Well," I finally reply. "I don't know what to say, Steve."

"I think this is very courageous of you, Steve," Bernie gently intervenes.

I'm perplexed. What is Bernie saying? Steve is sabotaging the whole effort, and Bernie is encouraging him. I feel angry, but Bernie's look tells me not to react quite yet.

"It's not easy to honestly share your opinion," Bernie continues addressing everyone. "And obviously there's a need alive in Steve that's not satisfied by the experiment that the rest of you are willing to engage in."

He turns to Steve.

"Would you like to tell us more about it, Steve?"

"What do you mean?" Steve asks, clearly uncomfortable by this question.

"I'm curious about what we can learn from you. What are you afraid of?" Bernie asks him. "For instance, what is the worst thing that could happen if you were to take part in this experiment and implement S3 patterns?"

Bernie seems to understand Steve. I feel my anger subsiding and I admire his approach.

Steve hesitates for a moment, but then goes on: "I don't believe that my people can solve all their problems themselves. That's precisely our task as managers, to maintain control and overview, and certainly to define the structure of the organization. My people don't yet have the maturity to think on that level, let alone organize themselves. Unless I manage them, things will definitely go wrong."

Bernie stays friendly and calm even after such strong assertions.

"Okay, so you're convinced that the people in your department need direction and that they're not yet capable of organizing themselves?"

Steve nods.

"That's okay, Steve, "Bernie assures him. "And at the same time, it makes me wonder about the actual needs behind your reaction. Are there organizational drivers at play to which you are unconsciously responding? Or maybe some of your personal needs are in danger because of this new approach to management? Or both?"

The room remains silent. Steve shifts uncomfortably back and forth on his seat. Just like me, he had not anticipated these questions.

"No idea," Steve finally says quietly.

"That's quite all right," Bernie answers. "For most of us, it is difficult to understand our needs and feelings, let alone express them in a group. So let's not dig into my last questions any deeper for now."

Bernie hesitates for a moment and adds: "But if you do want to talk about it some more, I'll be happy to. Both you and the organization could benefit from understanding the deeper layers beneath your decision not to participate in pulling in S3 patterns."

"Okay," Steve nods.

"Do you have any objections to us continuing with this?" Julia asks cautiously, seeking eye contact with Steve.

Bernie smiles at me. He's noticed how Julia is looking for consent by checking for any objections. It's typical of Julia to pick up new things quickly.

"No, I don't think so," Steve replies.

"Okay, Steve," I say. "And what, if anything, do you need from us? And how would you like to be involved? For example, I'm imagining that our weekly get-togethers will include a lot of S3 experiments from now on."

Steve reflects for a moment.

"For the moment, I don't need to be part of the weekly meetings, but I would like to be able to bring any questions or problems from my department to you guys. And certainly to you, Chris. Perhaps you and I can get together once a week for a status update?"

I'm slightly reluctant but I agree, on condition that he'll still attend our weekly meetings if there are specific topics that require his presence. And that he won't wait for a weekly status update with me to address specific questions or problems. I don't want to become a bottleneck. I also ask Steve to make sure that people from his team continue to have constructive conversations with the rest of the organization regarding questions people have, or dependencies and the like. I don't want Steve's department to become even more of a silo than it already is.

"So," Bernie steps in, concluding the conversation. "I get the sense that we could all do with a break. Is that right?"

Everyone nods. I could definitely do with a break. My legs are shaking. Steve's decision was tough for me to swallow. A little fresh air will do me good.

"Great," Bernie says. "Let's take 15 minutes. And then we will go on to look at the role of the spokesperson."

"Do I need to be back here after the break?" Steve asks.

I hesitate before responding: "I would really love you to join us in this experiment, Steve. But it's up to you to decide to come back to our meeting or not."

"Chris," Bernie says after all others have left the meeting room, "I wanted to check in with you briefly. How do you feel about what just happened? I can imagine Steve's reaction was rather unexpected."

"I'm a bit shaken by it, yes," I reply. "And I feel a bit angry about him quitting so early, without giving S3 a chance."

"I understand," Bernie says and then pauses for a moment. "I'm assuming that some kind of vulnerability lies beneath his decision, and the wish to take care of himself. And I guess also to take care of the well-being of HRS."

"Yeah," I sigh, "I'm convinced that Steve is really committed to the company and our products. And I know he's someone who needs time to change. I remember we once suggested that HR should be present at every job interview. Steve plainly refused at first. But now he won't be in any of these conversations without HR next to him. Just last month, he postponed an interview because no one from HR could be there."

Bernie nods.

"So I suppose this is all a bit fast for him," I reflect. "I really hope it is just a matter of time before he joins our experiments, but I doubt it. Steve and I have always had quite different opinions about how to create good software and manage our departments. That's no secret."

S3 is an invitation to develop a fundamentally different perspective on how we view ourselves and how we collaborate.

"You know," Bernie responds, "the change we're introducing isn't just about new tools or a new work agreement. It goes much deeper than that. S3 may offer us a collection of very useful patterns but above all else, it's an invitation to develop a fundamentally different perspective on how we view ourselves and how we collaborate. I also believe this is what HRS now needs."

"Yes, I think so too," I nod.

"And that's not easy for Steve," Bernie says. "But he might just need some time and the opportunity and support to grow into it. As soon as he sees concrete results coming out of our S3 experiments, he might be willing to join us."

"I hope you're right, Bernie," I say. "I really do."

"We'll have to see," he responds. "Would you mind if I spend some time with him to explore his needs and how he could address them more effectively? Only if he asks me to, of course."

"Not at all," I respond. "Although I don't think he'll ask you."

"You never know," Bernie smiles as we leave the meeting room to get some coffee.

14

ROLE SELECTION

When Julia and I arrive back in the meeting room, I'm surprised to see that Bernie has moved all the tables to the side and set up a circle of chairs in the room. He obviously enjoys our confused looks as we hesitantly try to find a place among the others in the circle.

"I understand you're not used to this, but look at it as an experiment," Bernie says. "A circle like this invites both equivalence and, by removing obstacles between us, also vulnerability and openness."

I'm uneasy about the fact that Steve is no longer with us. He didn't come back after the break. I feel guilty, as if it is my fault. The distance that has always existed between Steve and me now seems to be physically visible.

Sarah seems oblivious to this and enthusiastically takes the lead.

"Let's continue with the role of the spokesperson," she suggests. "Is there someone who'd like to take it on?"

"Wait a minute," Bernie stops her, laughing at her enthusiasm. "This is a great opportunity to use the role selection process. It's an S3 pattern designed to help you select a suitable person to take on a role. Actually, you can use it any time you want to decide between two or more options, but it's typically used for choosing someone for a role or to select one or more members for a team. In the role selection process, you don't start with a volunteer."

"Why not?" Julia asks. "Don't you want someone who's motivated to take on the role? You're not going to just designate someone?"

"Of course we want someone who's motivated to take on the role," Bernie agrees. "But what's the risk of working with volunteers?"

"They're always the first or the loudest to call out," Sarah says.

"Right," Bernie nods. "And perhaps this would be a good opportunity for someone else to learn and grow by taking on a certain role."

"But," Julia interrupts, "if you appoint someone, you don't always know whether that person is truly motivated."

"True," Bernie replies. "What's more, when a single person appoints someone, they have only part of the picture. So, as with using a volunteer, you miss out on tapping into the collective wisdom of the group. And coming to a more informed decision."

"The role selection process," he continues, "is based on nominations and consent. This way, you maximize the use of collective intelligence, and end up with motivated people being selected. Would you like me to guide you through the process? We could use it for selecting a spokesperson."

Everyone nods.

"Okay, let's start with the role domain description," Bernie begins. "In this case, we're already pretty close, given that we've neatly described the domain."

The role selection process maximizes the use of collective intelligence when selecting people.

He points to the flip chart. "The only thing left to do is to add a term, which is the period of time that someone may keep the role before a new role keeper is selected. This might mean a new person is chosen for the role next time, or the previous role keeper takes it again. It all depends whom the strongest argument is for."

"I think six months is a good term," Sarah calls out.

"What? Isn't that a bit short?" Peter asks.

"No," I interject, "it could be even shorter."

"But it depends who takes on the role, right?" Julia asks.

A discussion about the term ensues. Bernie smiles and lets us go on until he finally interrupts us a few minutes later.

"May I help you?" he asks. Without waiting for an answer, he continues. "I see you're diligently trying to reach consensus. I guess this could turn into a long conversation, and probably far longer than some of you would like. Right?"

No need to answer this question. We often have heated discussions where we talk over one another without really listening and coming to a conclusion. Often, Paul ended up making the decision if the conversation got stuck. "Do you remember I told you that consent is a very important principle in S3?" Bernie asks. "Well, I'll explain more about it later, but for now, I'd like to try to see whether we can reach consent about the term quickly. So I propose we go for a six-month term and set a review frequency of three months. This means that the person taking on the role gets feedback halfway through the term, at which point they set up a development plan."

Bart stops taking notes and looks inquisitively at Bernie. I notice how Carlos and Sarah also exchange quizzical looks.

"I know, that's a lot of information in a very short time." Bernie smiles. "But do you remember how we decided to set the review frequency in the domain description for three months? By setting the term of the role at six months, the role keeper organizes a peer review halfway through, as well as at the end of his term."

DEFINITION

An appointment to a role is always temporary, after which there is a reselection where the same role keeper may be chosen, or somebody new.

Bernie gives us a few seconds to let it sink in. When he feels we understand, he goes on: "So I propose that we choose six months as the term for the role of spokesperson. Does anyone have an objection? What I mean is, do you see any reason why this proposal could lead to consequences we'd rather avoid? Or how it could be easily improved in a worthwhile way?"

He looks around the room.

Peter wants to say something but decides otherwise. "Nothing major," he explains as Bernie gives him a questioning look.

I also shake my head. "Neither do I," I say.

None of the others has an objection either.

"Okay," Bernie says cheerfully. "Then we have a decision. That's how easy consent can be."

"Wait a minute," Julia says. "It can't always be that fast. Often people do have ideas or objections. What happens then?"

"Right," Bernie says. "That's why there's the Consent Decision Making pattern in S3, which helps a group to take a decision via a series of steps, and to deal with potential objections effectively and efficiently. But I'll explain this process in detail when we run into a decision that would benefit from it, okay?"

Julia looks reassured. I'm really happy that Bernie is here to teach us S3 step by step, based on what we need. Without him I'd have had no idea how to start.

"So," Bernie says, "as the role domain description is clear, we can begin with the next step of the role selection process: nominating a person to take on the role. Who is the most appropriate person? I'd like you all to explore your thoughts and feelings about this, considering the role domain description, of course. To avoid influencing one another, I want each of you to write the name of your nominee on a Post-it and keep it secret for now."

While we're reflecting and writing, Carlos asks: "What if I don't want to nominate anyone — or can't, for example, when there's no one with the right competencies or knowledge?"

"Then write "pass" on your Post-it," Bernie answers. "That's completely acceptable."

When everyone's done, Bernie goes on to the next step. He asks us to take turns to briefly share who we nominated and why. He points at Julia to start. "I nominated Chris, because he can best explain the new way of working that we're about to develop," Julia says. "Though I know he's not that keen on appearing before the media."

It's my turn next, and I explain that I've nominated Sarah because of her enthusiasm and her client focus as the sales and marketing manager. Sarah starts to protest but Bernie calmly asks her to hold back for now. He assures us that no one has to take on a role if he or she doesn't want to, and that we'll get into this in a moment.

Peter's next.

"I nominated myself," he says, looking hesitantly around the circle.

"That's perfectly fine," Bernie reassures him. "Why do you think you are the right person to take on the role?"

"I think that my financial background could generate trust with the media. And the fact that I'm on the board could help too," Peter replies.

Carlos has also nominated Peter, because he feels that he communicates clearly and writes well.

Sarah has a question mark on her Post-it. "I really had no idea who to nominate," she apologizes.

"That's also fine, Sarah," Bernie says. "And you, Bart?"

Bart turns his note around. My name is on it.

"Even though I think Peter is pretty well-suited to the role, I feel that Chris is the better candidate," he says. "I believe it makes sense for the CEO to be visible, and the world expects it. Which is exactly what Paul did."

"Okay," Bernie says. "Now we know all your nominations and arguments. The next step is to check if there is any additional information to add or to ask for. Does anyone have a question or would like to share something that could help us to make our decision?"

We look at each other awkwardly.

"There's no need to share or ask anything if nothing comes to mind right now," Bernie reassures us. "But if you have any valuable information that hasn't yet come up regarding this selection, or you'd like to ask about something particular, now is the time to do so."

"Yes." I hesitate for a moment. "I don't know whether it makes sense to share this, but I really don't feel like taking on the role. I always feel a bit uncomfortable in formal communication with the media, and I often can't find the right words."

"Okay," Bernie nods.

"Does anyone else have a question or would like to share something?" he asks, looking around the circle to my left and making eye contact with each person in turn.

Everyone indicates that they don't, until he gets to Sarah.

"I don't have a question or information about this role selection process," she says cautiously. "But I think I now understand better why you didn't want to start out with a volunteer."

Sarah looks probingly at Bernie as she finishes her sentence. He nods.

Encouraged, Sarah continues: "Not only would we miss out on a lot of information if we simply picked a candidate, but this process also allows us to give one another feedback. As much as I wouldn't want to take on that role, I really enjoyed the appreciation that Chris expressed in his explanation for my nomination."

"It was the same for me," I add. "And I can see how explaining the reasons for the nominations in this way can bring recognition and clarity. It also probably leads to greater support for the person who ends up taking on the role, right?"

I look at Bernie as I finish talking. He nods.

"Very true," he says. "That's why this is such a powerful pattern in S3. Often, after hearing the well-founded nominations of others, someone takes on a role that they would never otherwise have considered. As a result, they learn and grow a lot as a person too. To my mind, selecting people on the strength of the reason is a really great pattern to help people empower themselves."

The role selection process acknowledges all those who are nominated and maximizes support for the person who is selected.

Julia nods, delighted by this comment. She too seems to understand the potential of the process.

"But we're not done yet," Bernie says cheerfully. "So, let's go on. We've listened to the reasons behind your nominations and we've checked whether we're missing any additional information. Now, does anyone want to change their nomination based on what they've learned so far?" Bernie asks.

"You can do that?" I ask surprised.

"Of course," Bernie explains. "By listening to all the nominations and reasons, we've learned a lot and this can influence your opinion. Perhaps someone brought up strong arguments that you hadn't thought of until you heard them."

"Then I'd like to change my nomination," Sarah says.

"Okay," Bernie says. "So if any of you want to change your nomination, please write down the new name on your Post-it before we hear about it." Sarah crosses out her question mark and writes a name instead. I don't see anyone else writing anything though.

After a moment Bernie invites Sarah to speak.

"I think the argument that the spokesperson should be a member of the board is a strong one," she explains. "And I'd like to propose Paul, because he's been really good at it. Perhaps he would like to take on the role."

She looks at Bernie: "Can you propose someone outside this group?"

Bernie nods.

"Not a problem at all," he explains. "Although selecting Paul would only be an in-principle agreement until we check with him whether he would object to taking on the role."

"Did anyone else change their proposal?" Bernie asks.

No one responds and after waiting a moment, he continues: "In the next step, it's my responsibility as the facilitator to ensure that a nominee is proposed on the strength of the reasons given. I can do this in several ways. For example, if there are strong arguments for two or more nominees, I would invite those people to have a brief dialogue to decide between them who they would nominate for the role. Alternatively, I could invite dialogue between others too, or suggest any other sensible approach."

"But for now," Bernie says, "considering there are strong arguments for Peter, and that both Chris and Sarah indicated they wouldn't want the role, and because Paul isn't here and we don't know if he'd even take on the role anyway, I propose Peter for this role. For the next six months."

Peter smiles and straightens up. He is clearly happy with this proposal.

"The final step," Bernie goes on, "is to check whether there are any objections to having Peter take on the role of spokesperson. An objection is an argument that reveals a reason why this proposal would not be good enough for now or safe enough to try. Another way of thinking about it is to consider if choosing Peter would lead to consequences we'd rather avoid, or that there is an even stronger reason for someone else and you can explain why." Bernie hesitates for a moment, and then says: "Normally, we would use hand signals to show simultaneously whether you object to this proposal or not. But I'd rather explain these hand signals in more depth when we are using the consent decision-making process for the first time. So, today, I would simply like to ask whether anyone has an objection to Peter taking on the role of spokesperson, according to the role domain description we constructed and the term of six months we agreed upon?"

He looks around the circle.

"Any objections?" Bernie asks one more time.

We all shake our heads.

"No objection," Peter says.

"Awesome," Bernie smiles. "You've just completed your very first role selection."

Role Selection

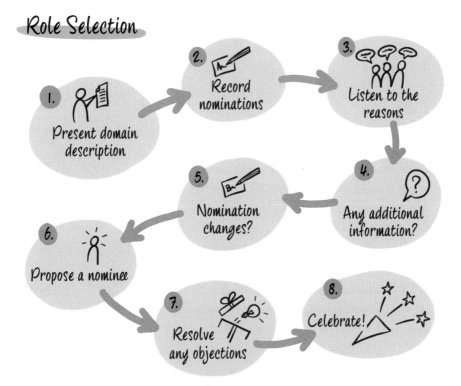

"Cool!" Sarah exclaims. "That was fast. What a great way to select someone for a role!"

"Exactly," Bernie says. "And I'd like to add a few more comments about the process before we go on. One matter is when somebody does have an objection to a proposed person. It's up to the facilitator to help the group deal with it and in the first instance it typically pays off to see if you can build on the existing proposal. This makes sense in many cases as there are often strong reasons for the person being proposed. Shortening the review frequency or making an amendment to a domain are two examples of how to resolve an objection without proposing someone else instead. But sometimes an objection cannot be resolved and then it's necessary to propose another nominee instead."

"And I would also like to add," he continues, "that we shouldn't forget to carry out a peer review in three months. How shall we remember to do this?"

"We can put it on our intranet," Carlos says.

"Hmm, yes, but that won't alert us when it's about time," Julia counters. "I'm afraid we might forget. Can't we just put it in someone's calendar?"

"Yes, sure, no problem," Peter says. "I'll do it myself, and have my calendar remind us of it in three months. Would that work?"

"Very good," Bernie says. "I suggest you bring it into this meeting at that time and we'll treat it as a driver just like any other."

"I will," Peter says, and takes his phone out to put it in his calendar immediately.

I suspect that there must be more convenient ways to remind ourselves about these peer reviews and the evaluation of agreements. I'm making a note to myself to look into a practical tool that can automate this.

We still have one driver on the flip chart that we haven't yet addressed, about changes needed to make HRS a more agile and effective company and to build great products once again.

"Pfff," Carlos sighs, "this will require more than just one role or agreement."

"True," Julia agrees. "And even a circle probably won't be enough because there are so many possible initiatives that fall under this driver. I assume that in addition to necessary changes in our product and development teams, we'll also need to adapt our HR procedures."

I nod. I too believe that this driver has a much broader and deeper impact than the previous ones. To respond to it effectively, we'll need to create a very different organization.

"Not by chance, S3 has a pattern for this as well," Bernie says. "I think this is a great opportunity to use Driver Mapping. It's a process you can use in a group to identify ways to begin responding to a complex problem. And in this case, we could use it to kickstart the development of our organizational structure, identifying some roles and circles we could put in place to help respond to this driver."

Bernie looks amused as he sees our confused looks.

"It's not as difficult as it seems," he explains. "You start with a group wishing to respond to an important and significant driver and then determine a number of likely subdrivers that need to be considered. You sort them into logical groups and in doing so, identify a number of smaller domains. After that, people take on initial responsibility for these domains by forming temporary circles and beginning to make decisions about how to proceed. Later on, you can decide on more specific roles and teams required to respond to the various drivers you identified. This is how you create an initial structure and organization to begin responding to the driver you started from."

I'm beginning to see more clearly now. Sarah, Carlos and Julia also nod, seemingly getting a better grasp of the concept.

"We could use driver mapping for addressing our third driver," Bernie says, pointing at the flip chart. "This is how we generate logical and workable domains for the larger changes that are necessary at HRS, and people from the whole organization can become actively involved in it."

I'm completely sold on this idea. To me, this seems an ideal approach to bringing S3 patterns into the organization in a natural way. I see Sarah nodding emphatically, apparently liking it too.

"This really sounds very interesting," Julia says. "But who will carry out this exercise? You can't do that with the whole organization. We are talking about 160 people."

"You're right," Bernie replies. "Although technically you could involve everyone for parts of the process, it works well with a smaller group – 30 to 40 people, for example. And it's very important that the group be as representative as possible of the whole of HRS."

"Wait a minute," Peter interjects, straightening up in his chair. "Are you implying that a random group of HRS employees will redefine the whole organization?"

His voice is louder than usual, and although he is directing his question at Bernie, he glances at me, as if expecting support from my side.

"Yes and no, Peter," Bernie says, maintaining composure. "I wouldn't recommend working with a random group, but only with employees who feel called to collaborate on creating the new HRS. Those who have the desire and the energy to reflect on the necessary changes at HRS to turn the ideas and structures that come out of the driver mapping into reality."

Peter interrupts Bernie again, even more firmly this time. He clearly doesn't think this is a good idea.

"And how exactly are you planning on selecting these people?"

"Well, you could work with nominations, just as we did for the role selection," Bernie answers calmly. "But given that this involves so many people, I don't think it's the most effective approach. I'd suggest you instead consider inviting the whole organization and see who's prepared to join the effort. 'Working with the willing', so to speak."

I admire his calmness. He obviously doesn't see Peter's questions as an attack on him or on S3. I would certainly have trouble with this if I were in his shoes.

"Change by invitation, as Chris explained to us last week," Carlos points out. I nod. Peter is quiet, but his expression shows that he doesn't buy it.

"Peter?" Bernie asks, not ignoring Peter's clear body language.

"No, nothing, just go on," Peter says.

"I'm still curious to hear what you think about it, Peter. Because you seem to disagree," Bernie says. "And it would be a shame not to benefit from the wisdom you can bring to this story."

"I just don't understand how you can keep control over what happens when you do things this way," Peter sighs after brief reflection.

He is looking at me as he says it, clearly hinting at my new role as CEO.

"What does S3 say about maintaining control as management?" Peter asks, this time to Bernie.

"Good question, Peter," Bernie says. "In fact, S3 leaves it up to you to determine the level of control, meaning that S3 doesn't impose complete autonomy. A circle is semi-autonomous. It gets its driver from the delegator, typically a superset circle, and operates within the constraints defined by its domain."

S3 doesn't impose anything. It is up to you to determine how much autonomy to give to individuals and groups.

"A superset circle?" Sarah asks.

"Yes," Bernie continues. "In S3 we speak of subset and superset circles. As the name implies, a subset signifies a group of smaller parts, whereas the superset refers to the larger, all-encompassing whole. So, when a circle decides within its domain to set up a new circle around one of its drivers, this new circle is the subset of the first circle, which then becomes its superset."

When he sees Sarah and a few others nod in understanding, Bernie continues: "Do you remember that we added a delegator to the domain description? The superset circle is the delegator since it is delegating autonomy and responsibility to the subset circle. When a new circle is created this way, the members of this subset circle, the delegatees, will define their strategy to respond to the driver of their circle and then seek consent on their strategy from their delegator. This is how the surrounding circle, the delegator, maintains overall accountability for the driver, the domain boundaries and the strategy of the subset circle."

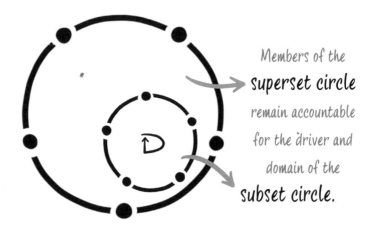

Members of the **superset circle** remain accountable for the driver and domain of the **subset circle.**

Again, Bernie is waiting to see whether his words have landed.

"This way, the management of an organization can ask a new circle to organize their work in a certain way or within certain constraints. For example, if required, they could ask a new circle to select a Coordinator to organize the work, or they may even select someone themselves. In this case, a coordinator would act a bit like a manager, but in the form of a role instead of a function, and only regarding the operations, because members of a circle would conduct governance together, just as we've been doing together this morning."

Peter nods. He seems somewhat reassured.

"Sometimes, this coordinator also becomes a representative of the superset circle, which is the delegator in this case," Bernie continues. "The goal is to maintain the delegator's interests and influence in the subset circle when it comes to making important decisions. And you could also combine that with bringing in a representative of the subset circle who participates in the delegator's governance meetings, representing the needs of the subset circle in decisions being made in the superset circle. This is called Double Linking."

"Cool" Julia responds, beaming. "That's how you make sure that someone from whatever circle can bring his driver into the largest, all-encompassing circle, if necessary. Now I also understand better what you mean by equivalence throughout the whole organization."

"Exactly, Julia," Bernie says. He realizes that not everyone understood what Julia was saying. "But you don't need to grasp all the details of this quite yet. You'll soon discover which circles and roles will be emerging at HRS and how they can be linked with representatives, based on the apparent needs." We nod.

Only Peter reacts: "Okay, but if S3 leaves it up to us to determine the level of governing and control, what are we going to decide around that?"

"I really want to give a lot of autonomy to our people," I say. "As I told you last week, I would like HRS to continuously adapt and renew itself. And I want the employees to be intrinsically motivated and build great products with us. I believe that to do so, we need to give teams or individuals as much autonomy as possible. At least, if that's what they want. Not 'bosses' who micromanage and constantly look over everyone's shoulders. We have to dare to give freedom and trust to our people, in exchange for transparency, motivation and a greater sense of responsibility."

"Which doesn't mean that you will lose your overview or even control," Bernie adds. He points at the flip chart and the drawing he made earlier. "Because in a company such as yours, everything remains in service of the primary driver of the organization. All other drivers, and the roles and teams that respond to them too, are in service of that primary driver, which is the sole reason for them to exist in the organization in the first place."

We must dare to give freedom and trust to our people, in exchange for transparency, motivation and a greater sense of responsibility.

Peter seems satisfied. And I gained more insight and confidence in how S3 can be applied in HRS.

"Okay," Peter says. "I think I more or less understand the concept. Though it still needs to sink in a bit."

Carlos, Bart and Sarah nod.

"Of course," Bernie says. "This is a lot of information in a very short time. And the driver mapping workshop could be a good next step to integrate all these insights in a practical way."

No one objects, and we decide that during the all-hands meeting next Friday we'll call for motivated volunteers to participate in the driver mapping exercise. Bernie and I will pick a date and make all the practical arrangements. Bernie will facilitate the workshop, and we'll all actively participate.

We finish our meeting with a closing round, to check in again with ourselves and briefly share what's alive in us or how we feel about the meeting. I'm surprised that everyone seems to be quite happy and positive, though most of us also indicate that there was a lot of information given within a short period of time, which still has to sink in some more.

What satisfies me most is that Peter sounds more optimistic when it's his turn to speak. I really hope that he'll continue to support this project. Given his role as financial director and his seat on the board, this is really important.

15

THE HONEST STORY

"What's the matter, sweetheart?" Kate asks me. "You've been in a bad mood all morning."

It's Thursday morning and I'm working from home so I can concentrate on preparing for tomorrow's all-hands meeting.

"Sorry, sweetheart, it's got nothing to do with you," I explain. "Tomorrow we have the meeting that I told you about. Paul's going to tell everyone why HRS urgently needs change and why he's resigning as CEO. And then I'll have to explain my ideas about the changes I think are necessary. That's why I'm putting a presentation together. It kept me awake half the night."

Kate raises her eyebrows.

"Oh my, that's not the Chris I'm used to," she says.

"No, I know. But I've no idea how to bring this across in a clear way. The whole company seems anxious about the direction I want to take HRS. I'll have to come up with a strong story tomorrow, or else I'll be in trouble."

Kate gives me a hug and I relax a little.

"Aren't you making a bigger deal out of this than it really is, Chris?" she asks. She looks concerned and sits down next to me. "How do you know the whole company is anxious? Most people at HRS like you very much. I'd imagine that they'll be rather curious about what you'll tell them."

"Four project leaders have already asked me whether it is true that I intend to get rid of all management functions. Of course, it's not true, but where will it end if rumors like this are making the rounds?"

"And what do your former teams think of it?" Kate asks.

"Well, they seem to like it. They're even looking forward to the potential of seeing more self-organizing teams in the future. But they already know me very well, so that doesn't really count."

"Okay, and who else was complaining?" Kate asks.

"Well, nobody really. Only the project managers. And Steve, of course. He's been running around like a nervous wreck all week."

"Which makes sense, given that he decided not to participate in the S3 experiment. Did he cause problems this week?" Kate asks.

"No, not at all," I admit. "He just walks around nervously and sticks even more closely to his people and the planning than before."

"So, Steve is nervous and four of the 160 people are anxious." Kate puts her hands on her hips and makes a serious face. "And our Chris here thinks that the whole world is against him and that he's not good enough."

I laugh, albeit a bit half-heartedly.

"What's the most convincing thing you could do tomorrow?" Kate asks me.

"Desperately try to put on the best slideshow ever and persuade everyone with an impressive story in which you promise that everything will turn out for the best?"

"No," I sigh, and I close my laptop, "because I don't know whether everything will turn out for the best."

"Exactly, and there's no way you can take on that responsibility anyway. That's the old way of thinking, that CEOs are personally accountable for everything. What you want is for everyone to take responsibility for themselves and have an impact together."

I sigh.

"You're right, Kate," I admit after a moment of reflection.

"How about you let go of making beautiful slides for tomorrow and simply tell your story instead?" Kate says. "Explain things exactly as they are, including your insecurities and doubts. It is very powerful when a CEO shows his vulnerability and acknowledges to his employees that he doesn't have all the answers. This way, you'll show you firmly believe in a new way of working and you want to set the example."

Kate pauses and looks at me intensely.

"Didn't you tell me that invitation-based change requires everyone, and especially you as a leader, to set an example with your behavior and act in the way you'd like others to act?" she asks.

"Yes," I nod. "This is even a pattern in S3, called Be the Change."

"Perfect, so then you'll join me for the yoga class?" she asks cheerfully.

I look at my computer, hesitating for a moment, but then decide to accept her proposal. I'll tell my story honestly without any fancy slides, just like I did in the management team meeting. It worked well there...

16

THE ALL-HANDS MEETING

"Good morning, dear colleagues," I pick up from Paul, who has been telling everyone what was going on at HRS and why he's passing the baton to me. Almost all HRS employees showed up for the all-hands meeting, looking at me with great anticipation as I step onto the stage. I follow my gut feeling and decide to run with the idea I had in the shower this morning. I don't just want to tell them where I want to go with HRS, but for them to feel it too.

"Paul just outlined very well why we need to change things at HRS in order to survive," I start off. "And as you may have heard here and there in the corridors, I'm happy to take on that challenge. However, not in a typical top-down reorganization as many of you might have experienced in traditional company settings. I want to change course together with you, and invite you to help reinvent our processes and organization step by step yourselves. But before I get into this, I'd like you to experience what I mean."

I look around the room to make eye contact with Bernie. He smiles at me. I ask everyone to move the chairs to the side and to stand anywhere in the room. Then I ask them to randomly choose two colleagues out of the group, without indicating this to them.

"Good," I continue when I see that everyone is done. "So, how long will it take for me to put you in a nice equilateral triangle with the two colleagues that you've just chosen?"

"All of us?" someone from Carlos's department shouts out above the murmur. "The whole day. That's a lot of triangles!"

"I think so too," I say as the noise settles down again. "If it wasn't an impossible task, it would take me all day. But that's what is often expected of CEOs or managers — to keep track of all their employees, take care of the planning and make sure that everyone is doing what he or she should be doing, right?"

There's much nodding and murmuring throughout the room.

"Let's see what happens if I let you organize yourselves instead. These are your triangles after all, not mine. So, move around and quietly form your triads, so you're standing at equal distance from the other two people you've chosen. Do it silently, please, and without showing your two colleagues that you've chosen them. Go ahead."

Some people are reluctant to move, but soon everybody is milling around the room. I'd learned this approach in a course about the Scrum framework for product delivery, albeit with a smaller group. I'm hoping it will work here too, in such a large group.

After a while, the movements slow down and everyone stands still. It took less than two minutes.

"You see, you're much better at organizing yourselves than I could ever be," I resume. "The triads that you're now standing in are a metaphor for working together with a colleague, client or supplier, or your entire team. They're also representative of the countless possible relationships and ways to collaborate that exist in a company such as ours.

You are in it with both feet every single day and feel whatever is needed at any given moment. No manager will ever be able to sense these needs as quickly and competently as you can. And you are strong and powerful when you find a stable, but not rigid, position in your triangles."

No manager will ever be able to sense these needs as quickly and competently as you can.

I walk around among the employees and ask some colleagues to take a different position in the room.

"Moving these people represents changes or disturbances in our system. Something unexpected could happen in our market or with a client, or even internally in our organization. You are the ones who can adapt incredibly quickly and effectively to such a change, and much faster than I could direct you to do as the CEO. So, now that things have changed in our system, try to form your triangles again."

The milling begins anew, and this time it takes less than a minute for everyone to find a new position, forming a triangle with their two colleagues. "Have you noticed something?" I ask them. "There are countless triad positions possible, and you very quickly found a new, stable position. This is what makes you both strong and resilient at the same time. You're organizing yourselves, which is exactly what we will need at HRS in the future. This is why autonomy will need to become one of our core values."

I ask everyone to sit down again and begin to speak openly and honestly — about how Paul asked me to take over his role and how my encounter with Bernie gave me the courage to take on this challenge. I explain how I want to see the organization function as a living system and what I believe is needed to accomplish this.

Using a flip chart, I explain briefly and concisely the S3 principles and some important concepts and patterns, such as drivers, domains, roles and circles. "I know this may all sound a bit fuzzy to you," I say. "But I did want to introduce you to S3 and to give you the feeling that S3 can help us to become a new kind of organization, which reinvents itself continuously, adapting efficiently and effectively to every change as you just demonstrated in the exercise. And all of this will help us to support our clients and our business in the best possible way."

To make it a bit more concrete, I ask someone from the management team to share something about the first steps we've taken with S3. Sarah rises to the occasion and enthusiastically relates how, together with Bernie, we described the most important drivers for our team and responded to them by choosing Peter as the spokesperson and by organizing a driver mapping workshop.

While Sarah speaks, I place the sheet with the driver that we'd identified together for the driver mapping on the flip chart: *"Due to the current structure and culture at HRS, we're confronted by a number of problems such as demotivation, slow decision making and ineffective collaboration between teams. This has prevented us from launching version 4.0 successfully, and puts HRS at risk. We need to become more agile and effective as an organization, so that we can create and deliver awesome products again in the near future."*

"Thank you, Sarah," I say after she's finished. I turn to the room again and point to the driver summary on the board.

"As I just said, a driver is a person or a group's motive for responding to a specific situation. An organizational driver relates to some kind of need or opportunity the organization faces. This particular driver is currently the most important one HRS faces. As you can see, we've described it in a couple of sentences that summarize what's happening at HRS today including the consequences of that, and what we think is needed. This is the reason that Paul asked me to take over his role."

I pause deliberately to allow everyone time to absorb the driver.

"So, I'd like to invite you all to work with us so that together we can develop an effective response to this driver," I continue. "I'm convinced that the mindset and patterns coming from S3 can help us with that, and I'd ask you to experiment with them whenever you think they may be useful.

As a management team, we intend to support you in every way we can. I expect that successful experiments will spread, and the less successful ones will disappear, just as they do in nature. So, don't be afraid to experiment and learn through doing. It is our failures as well as our successes that will help us learn and develop new ways of working together to grow a more powerful and agile organism to make outstanding products for ourselves and our clients."

Just as in nature, successful experiments will spread, and less successful ones will become extinct.

After leaving a moment of silence to let my words sink in, I go on:
"One experiment we have already planned is the driver mapping workshop that Sarah talked about. It'll take place on Wednesday next week and anyone who wants to join us to work on that is most welcome. I'll send you all an invitation with more details."

I look around the room, trying to assess how my words have affected the group. I see many happy, enthusiastic faces, but also some concerned looks. Here and there a whisper.

"I understand that what I have given you today isn't very concrete," I continue. "No doubt, many questions will emerge in the coming days. We will be able to answer some of them immediately, others not. That will be our joint adventure and you can rely on the management team to actively accompany you on this journey. You can always come to us with questions or ideas."

I wrap up my presentation: "What are your most important questions at this point?"

Noah, an architect in Steve's department, is the first one to raise his hand.

"Why isn't Steve here?" he asks. His tone tells me that he has already picked up the answer in the corridors, but wants to check my reaction.

"I'm glad that you have asked that question, Noah," I answer. "I would have liked to have had Steve here today, but he decided not to be part of the S3 experiment in the management team for now. Some of you might have sensed that. Steve has strong doubts about the direction I want to take HRS and you. And I'm happy that he had the courage to stand up to me and the rest of the team. We can all learn from that."

"I have recently become a strong believer in change by invitation rather than by obligation," I continue. "Therefore I won't impose anything on Steve. I intend to use my authority as CEO as minimally as possible. What I will keep an eye on, as CEO, is that the most important drivers of HRS, such as this one, are being recognized and responded to."

I point to the flip chart with the driver summary.

"I also expect each department and team to keep this driver in mind and to contribute as best as they can, each in their own way."

There's agitation in the room. They clearly hadn't expected this answer.

"Believe me," I try to calm them down. "This is just as new and scary to me as it is to you."

"What will happen to our department? Will we continue to work in the old way?" Noah asks. The murmuring stops. Everyone seems to wait for my answer.

"I honestly don't know, Noah." I look him straight in the eye. "I believe that Steve has the best intentions for HRS and respect his choice. I hope that he and all of us will be able to evolve step by step, but let's wait and see what happens in the coming weeks. Let's also have the courage to be open and honest about any challenges that might arise."

Noah's expression tells me that he is satisfied with my answer. But I want to push it a bit further and look around the room.

"I don't know what's going to happen in the near future, and I won't have answers to many of your questions. And that is okay, as it is part of letting go of any apparent control that a manager or CEO is assumed to have. We need to learn to continuously inspect and adapt as we go, and stop sticking to detailed plans when they have long been made obsolete by new realities." The room is quiet.

"Any more questions that I don't know the answer to?" I ask, smiling.

A woman whose name I don't know — I think she is from Julia's team — speaks up: "You said that we can go ahead and experiment with S3. How can we find out more about it? And how much time do we have to invest in it?"

"Good question," I say. "And there I can give you a clever answer."

I hear people giggle.

"I hope," I say while glancing at Bernie, "that Bernie will be kind enough to give a few short workshops or training sessions about S3 in the coming weeks. This will help you to become familiar with S3, and you'll get some necessary background to dive into your first experiments."

Bernie gives this the thumbs up.

"And as to your second question," I continue, "I'd like to go back to the S3 principles."

I go over to the flip chart and look for the sheet on which I'd written the seven principles during my talk.

"Try to answer your own question based on these principles. Who has to make the decision on how much time you'll invest in experimentation?" I look around the room, curious as to what might come up.

"Based on equivalence, I gather that we can decide that ourselves," says the woman who asked the question.

"As long as we are transparent about it," someone chimes in.

I nod.

"Exactly. Equivalence means that everyone who is affected by a decision can also influence that decision. Thus, if the investment remains within your team or project, you decide together with your teammates. But if you want to invest a certain amount of time or money that will impact other teams or HRS as a whole, I'd expect you to include these other people in your decision-making process."

"Does this answer your question?" I ask the woman. She nods.

Bernie steps in: "I'd like to add something here. There are two other S3 principles linked to this question: working empirically and continuously improving. In order to apply these principles, you'll want to keep your experiments as small and low-cost as possible, continuously evaluating and adapting them as you go. Investments don't have to be heavy — on the contrary, in fact."

"Thank you, Bernie, good point."

I turn to the room again.

"So, as you can see, I'm also learning about S3 every day. Any more questions?"

Liam, a promising young developer, raises his hand.

"If equivalence is one of the basic principles, then why do we still need a management team?"

"I think you raise a good point, Liam," I answer. "Honestly, I don't think that we will still need managers in the traditional sense of the word. In this new paradigm, projects and products still need to be managed, of course, but people learn how to manage themselves. So, we can look forward to retirement pretty soon."

In this new paradigm, projects and products still need to be managed, but people learn to manage themselves.

I wink at Liam, and hear laughter in the group.

"No, I'm joking, of course," I explain. "We're not planning on retirement just yet, because even if we'll be managing people a lot less, I do think that we'll still have an important role to play. For example, we'll always need people to think about purpose, strategy and priorities at the company level, and we have a lot of experience in managing a company, which we can share with you. These are important drivers for the current management team to be taking responsibility for as we move ahead."

"Just because we're all equivalent," I continue, "doesn't mean that we all have to be equal and do the same kind of work. Everyone has his or her unique talents and interests. Besides, it would be no fun taking strategic decisions with 160 people. This is the power of small teams who can decide and act for themselves in response to the drivers they're responsible for. At the same time, equivalence lies in the fact that from now on every one of you can directly influence the decisions we take in the management team. If one of our choices creates a problem somewhere in the organization, this is a driver that needs to be addressed. Each driver should end up being dealt with by the right person or group. This is how your concerns or objections about a certain strategy could end up with us, and we'll deal with it. After all, why would we want to go ahead with certain decisions, when they create impediments elsewhere in the organization?"

I look around the room.

"Does that make sense?" I ask, pausing for a moment before continuing. "You know, this is really important to me. No one is better or more important than the other. We all have our unique talents and passions and therefore our own role to play in the whole story. And if strategy is a passion of yours, Liam, then perhaps you'd like to join us."

"No, thanks," Liam laughs, along with everyone else in the room, and I decide that this is a good moment to bring things to an end.

"So, I want to close this meeting with a request," I say. "I'd like to invite you in the coming days to pay attention to any tension you find yourself experiencing in the course of your daily work, and consciously consider what lies behind it. If you become aware of problems or opportunities that concern this organization, make it your responsibility to act on it. Up until now, we have put aside such things all too often, in the hope that someone else will pick them up and deal with them. Instead, please check where the drivers that you discover belong. Is it yours to take on? If so, then I hope that you'll take care of it. This is called accountability, remember? And if it belongs somewhere else, then bring it to the attention of that person, team or department, including us if you think it concerns me or the other managers. We are happy to learn from you about what is really important."

"Our intention," and I point again to the sheet with the driver, "is to create a more efficient and agile HRS. The next release of our product will be crucial for that. If version 5.0 of our product is unsuccessful, our company will be at serious risk."

I pause deliberately. It's essential for everyone to grasp the urgent need for this change.

"So, let's make this a success together, without any 'musts' or obligations. Whoever feels the energy to contribute to this change is welcome next Wednesday morning. But there are other and equally valuable ways to take initiative, for example, within your own team. I really believe that together we can create something beautiful and I look forward to achieving that with you."

A group of employees stays on after the all-hands meeting to chat. I listen eagerly to their questions and stories and realize that my message has landed pretty well. I was able to instill a sense of urgency in them, and they also seem to grasp what kind of change I have in mind. Some are outright enthusiastic, though most of them don't seem to know how to feel about all this, which is okay for now.

A group of five employees from the development team, all excited, come to talk to Sarah and I about the sales and marketing of version 4.0. They have many questions about it, and it's only now that I understand how little we involve them in the sales process, even though they know the product so much better than anyone else. What's more, they know the client better than Sarah and I had suspected. From their stories, I realize that during the development phase, they created a completely different type of contact with our clients than our sales people did. We failed to leverage their insights and experience to improve our product.

As I excuse myself, leaving them with Sarah so I can listen to another group, I notice that Peter has already left, although the management team had agreed that we would stay to answer all the questions.

That's strange, I think.

17

GOVERNANCE AND OPERATIONS

It's Monday morning, and we're sitting together as a management team. Bernie is with us again. Steve is not, which still feels strange to me. So I share that feeling during the check in as we begin the meeting.

Julia, Carlos and Sarah express their satisfaction with our last management meeting and the all-hands meeting. Sarah also tells us that she feels energized after introducing the check in with her people, who seem to find it quite useful. Bart explains that he's tired today because of a bad night, and that he has been consciously thinking about the drivers behind things he's been doing and questions he's been asked. Peter says that he's read something about S3, but that he has not yet seen an opportunity to put it into practice.

"Bernie," Julia asks after our opening round, "which S3 patterns are you going to teach us today?"

Bernie smiles broadly. "I suggest that I teach you something about how to organize your work and how to come to group decisions as effectively as possible. Therefore — just as we did last week — we should first look at the drivers that are currently relevant to you and tackle those. Okay?"

Everyone nods. I hesitate for a moment, but then ask: "I'd like to briefly share something on the practical side. May I? Or do I have to summarize a driver for it first?"

"Of course," Carlos grins. "And also first ask for written approval."

He winks at me and we all laugh.

"Okay," I say. "I just wanted to tell you that I've come to some clear agreements with Paul about the transfer of his role and work to me. He'll remain active here for as long as it takes to deliver version 4.0. It's almost ready, and with a bit of luck, it can be delivered as early as this week."

A sigh of relief goes around the table. Everyone understands the importance of being able to bring version 4.0 to completion and provide it to our clients, despite a delay of more than three months.

"Paul will continue to work on version 4.0 to handle initial customer service issues and potential questions from clients until it's stable enough to go into maintenance mode," I continue. "This will allow all of us to focus fully on the necessary organizational changes and on version 5.0. Which I'm incredibly grateful for, by the way."

"Also, during this period he'll help me with the daily duties I'm expected expected to fulfill as CEO, which I haven't mastered yet. He'll hand over to me whatever really belongs to me in the role of CEO and we'll delegate everything else. This means you'll see Paul around for a while longer, although he won't come to our meetings, to give us all the freedom we need. This will also make it clear to him — and probably to us too — that he's stepped out of his role as CEO. But Paul really wants to help us transition as quickly as possible. So, don't hesitate to involve him where necessary. In any case, he's staying on as a member of the board to support us from there."

I gesture toward Bernie to let him know I'm done.

"Would anyone like to respond to this before we move on?" he asks. Everyone shakes their head.

"A really great guy, that Paul," Carlos says, more to himself than to us. We all nod.

———

"Perfect," Bernie says. "Then I'd like you to get in touch with your bodies by putting your feet on the ground and taking a deep breath."

Bernie smiles, ignoring the restless shuffling of some members of the group and the awkward glances. He waits patiently until we've centered ourselves. I understand how new and revolutionary such little things are in a team like ours, which probably applies to most other teams at HRS as well. We're conditioned to use only our minds and show our rational side at work. And it is true for me too: although I've been doing yoga in my free time for years, I hardly ever talk about it at work.

I'm happy that Bernie introduces this practice with us so natural- *We're conditioned to use* ly, and I promise myself that I will do the same more frequently *only our minds and show* in future. *our rational side at work.*

"Feel what's alive in you at the moment," Bernie calmly continues. "What's happening in you or around you? Where is your attention? Are there things happening in the organization that call for action or a decision in this group?"

Bernie gives us time to reflect in silence and then asks us to summarize the drivers we discovered in a few words and write them each on a Post-it note. While we're writing, he puts two flip chart sheets on the wall and draws three columns on each of them. At the top of the left sheet, he writes, "Operations Board" and on the right one, "Governance Board".

Bernie asks us to take turns to explain our drivers to the group. Carlos is the first to speak.

"I have to double-check the hardware and other infrastructure items for version 4.0 with Paul and Steve this week," he explains.

"Great," Bernie nods. "And how would you describe that as a driver summary?"

Carlos gives Bernie a puzzled look.

"What is happening? And what is needed?" Sarah comes to his aid.

"Ah, right," Carlos nods. "There's a good chance that version 4.0 will finally go into production this week or early next week. And although we are pretty much prepared for it, we still need to do a last-minute check of all hardware and infrastructure to be absolutely sure that everything works the way it should. For that I need the help of Paul and Steve — and perhaps also yours, Chris."

I nod at Carlos.

"Interesting," Bernie says. "Is this something for which there is a need for a conversation or a decision in this group? Or is this work that is clearly understood and ready to be executed within existing agreements?"

"The latter," Carlos said. "The procedures and specifications are clear. The three or four of us simply have to do it this week."

Bernie sticks Carlos's Post-it onto the left sheet. "Then this is a perfect example of an operations driver. In S3, Operations means doing the work and organizing day to day activities within the constraints defined through governance. Therefore, when responding to an operations driver, you can immediately get to work because all necessary agreements or procedures have been decided on earlier."

"Does anyone else have a driver for the operations board?" Bernie asks.

"I do," Sarah pipes up. "At least I think so. After the all-hands meeting with Chris, I received feedback from some of the developers that it would be very useful to involve them more closely in our sales activities. This week, I'd like to free up some time to bring the developers in closer contact with the sales and marketing people to see how we can take some steps in that direction."

"Yes, this also seems to be an operations driver," Bernie agrees. "Or is there still something that we need to make a decision on together?"

"No," Sarah replies. "I've already talked to Chris and Steve about it. Both think this is a good plan, and they'll ask their developers to support the initiative. The question actually came from them, so we don't expect any problems."

"Great," Bernie responds. "And for us as a group, is this more important or less important than Carlos's driver?"

Everyone agrees with Sarah's assessment that Carlos's driver about the infrastructure of version 4.0 is more important and urgent at the moment.

"Good," Bernie nods, and he sticks Sarah's Post-it below that of Carlos.

"Let's prioritize this list of operations drivers from top to bottom. Prioritize Backlogs, as this would be called in S3."

"A backlog?" Julia asks. "Don't your teams use that too, Chris?"

I nod.

"Sure. This is a typical element in agile development methods. In Scrum, for example, you have a 'product backlog', which lists all the parts of a product that you're going to build. A Backlog is a transparent to-do list for the team, containing all uncompleted items. This list should be consciously prioritized and made visible to everyone. This creates clarity and focus."

"You might also want to set up a backlog for HR activities in your team, Julia," I add, "without having to implement the rest of Scrum or other agile practices right away."

"Right," Bernie says. "That's why a number of agile and lean techniques have been adopted as patterns in S3. These help teams to plan and implement their work more effectively. And S3 is modular, remember? This means that none of the S3 patterns is mandatory, and you can easily choose between them or adapt them, or combine them with other techniques."

"Now I understand why Paul chose you as CEO, Chris," Julia says admiringly. "You've been doing this kind of thing with your teams for years!"

I begin to blush. "No big deal. A few parts, but only on a team level. I'm really happy that Bernie is here to teach us about S3 and to help us implement patterns on an organizational level."

"Let's keep going," Bernie proposes, pointing at the sheet with the operations board. "This board is an easy but effective way to Visualize Work, and in this case visualize the status of all operations drivers that are on your operations backlog. I'm sure that you'll find better ways or tools to manage your backlogs later, but this is good enough for a start."

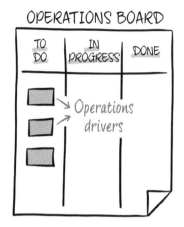

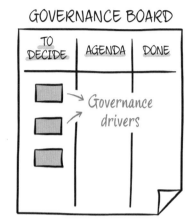

"And what about that other sheet?" Bart asks.

"That's your first governance board, visualizing your Governance Backlog," Bernie replies. "In S3, governance means setting objectives, and continuously making and evolving decisions that guide people towards achieving them."

Bernie pauses a while for his words to sink in.

"Governance drivers are drivers that require some kind of decision to be made that will govern future decisions and activity," he explains.

"Aha," Julia interrupts him. "In that case, our driver for selecting Peter for the role of spokesperson was also a governance driver?"

Bernie nods.

"Then all the drivers that we sorted out last week were governance drivers, weren't they?" Sarah asks.

"Two of them were," Bernie says. "But what about the driver concerning the communication about Paul's resignation in the all-hands meeting? Was that governance or operations?"

"Wasn't it an operational driver?" asks Julia.

"Yes it was," Bernie confirms.

Seeing our perplexed faces, Julia continues: "It's operational because that decision didn't…"

She pauses for a moment, looking at Bernie: "How did you put it? Ah yes, govern future decisions or activity."

"Exactly," Bernie reassures her. "If a driver requires a decision to be made but the decision won't constrain future decision making or the work that people do, then it's an operational driver. These kinds of decisions fall into the category of organizing work, which, in this case, Chris took on."

DEFINITIE

Governance is the act of setting objectives, and making and evolving decisions that guide people towards achieving them.

Sarah, Julia and Carlos show that they understand, and Peter says that he's now clear about the difference between governance and operations.

"Don't role keepers do governance at times?" Bart asks. "They also have to make some decisions that shape or constrain future decisions and work, don't they?"

"A very good question, Bart," Bernie says. "You are completely right. For a role, the difference between governance and operations is perhaps a bit less defined than within a circle. But as a role keeper, you also make decisions about which objectives you want to achieve, and you set your own constraints. And it makes sense to evaluate the agreements that you make with yourself on a regular basis, so you might write significant decisions down so you can come back to them later."

When I see that there are no further questions to Bernie's answer, I give him one of my Post-its.

"I still have an operations driver," I say. "Since not all HRS employees were at the all-hands meeting, I think it's really important that they hear the same story. So, I'd like to summarize and communicate what was said there. It'll also be a good reminder for everyone that was present in the all-hands meeting, of course."

Everyone agrees that this belongs to the operations backlog as well, and we decide that in terms of priority, this should be placed between the two other drivers. The infrastructure for version 4.0 stays on top.

The other drivers on our Post-its all seem to be governance drivers that require reflection and group decisions. We stick them onto our governance board, and prioritize them.

"Let's have a look at how circles handle their governance drivers," Bernie says.

He proceeds to tell us that it's useful to go over the governance backlog on a regular basis to address the most important items. This typically takes place in a governance meeting that's scheduled every two to four weeks, often at fixed intervals. Though Bernie explains that governance decisions are sometimes made on the go as well, especially in teams that are co-located and can afford to take time out of their day when needed. During governance meetings, the members of a circle jointly make and evolve the agreements needed to fulfill their objectives and take care of whatever governance issues come up in the course of their work.

Bernie teaches us what a governance meeting should look like. He recommends using the Prepare for Meetings pattern. This includes drawing up an agenda in advance by adding the drivers that require a conversation or a decision in the group to the governance backlog. We should also immediately prioritize the drivers, with the most important ones on top so they are the first ones to be processed during the meeting.

Thorough preparation of the governance meeting is crucial.

Bernie explains that whoever puts the driver on the backlog would be best suited to suggest how much time they consider valuable to dedicate to this agenda item. He should also add the patterns or approaches that are needed to address it effectively, and include details of any prerequisites to prepare. This could be important information to review before the meeting, what people to talk to, or more details about the driver. He also reminds the others to include evaluation of existing agreements in the agenda when they reach their evaluation date.

"It's important to prepare the governance meeting as thoroughly as possible," Bernie concludes. "At The Facts, we send an invitation in advance, with a list of all the drivers we'll be working on. We ask everyone to study or prepare in whatever ways are necessary, to make the best use of our time in the governance meetings."

Bernie outlines the flow of a governance meeting: "We begin with a check in. After that, we deal with a few administrative issues, such as consent about any minutes from the previous governance meeting and fixing a date for the next one."

"That's smart," Bart comments. "That way, you don't have to do that at the end when everyone is distracted or needs to rush off to the next appointment."

Bernie nods.

"Once that's done, we also check whether there are any objections to the planned agenda. Sometimes there are last-minute drivers coming in, or a change in priorities, so this is the moment when you can adjust your agenda accordingly."

"Hmm, that's quite a bit of preparation before you even start the meeting," Peter observes.

"Right," Bernie says. "However, coming prepared for the meeting and spending time at the beginning to check in and handle those administrative matters ensures that everyone is there, fully engaged, and that the meeting can run effectively and efficiently. You actually save time by doing so."

"When I visited The Facts, I was really surprised by how much work you accomplished in a single meeting," I confirm, looking at Bernie. "Some of those decisions were really difficult too. And you maintained a harmonious and constructive atmosphere throughout the meeting."

"The atmosphere in our meetings isn't a problem," Peter jumps in defensively.

"No, not at all," Carlos chuckles. "Sometimes it's so friendly that we forget to focus on our work entirely."

"Or we're so determined that we get into fights," Sarah adds.

Peter's about to say something else, but Bernie steps in quickly.

"That's exactly why it helps to facilitate these meetings and to choose a Governance Facilitator to guide the group through the agenda. Remember, each agenda item has a suggested timebox and a recommendation as to which patterns to use to deal with it, so the facilitator facilitates any necessary processes according to the time available. He also supports the group to keep conversations on track and maintain a constructive atmosphere throughout the meeting."

"Would that always be the same facilitator?" Julia asks.

"Or do we need someone from outside the group?" I add to her question.

"There are no hard and fast rules about it," Bernie says. "Sometimes a group might ask someone external to facilitate, as in our case today. But typically a facilitator is selected by the group, from the group, for the group. And it's often helpful to choose someone to keep the role for a period of time because they build familiarity with the governance board and the current state of its various drivers. But that doesn't mean that they facilitate all of the items. As you become familiar with S3 patterns and the flow of a governance meeting, you can often alternate between participation and facilitation where everyone takes turns to facilitate part of the meeting. Or you can spontaneously nominate someone to facilitate each time. It's up to you to decide."

"If everyone facilitates once in a while," Bernie continues, "it becomes easier over time. Because then everyone realizes how difficult facilitation can be at times, and you constantly help each other, especially in the context of artful participation."

"In the context of what?" Sarah asks. I'm also unsure sure what Bernie means.

"Oops," Bernie says as he sees our confused looks. "Didn't I explain artful participation to you last week? Then I'll do so as we work on our drivers, okay?"

We nod.

"So," Bernie picks up from before, "once there's a facilitator and the administrative items are dealt with, you can begin with the actual governance work. Usually, you start with any necessary short reports."

"Reports?" I ask.

"Yes," Bernie explains. "This is a moment to share information concerning relevant topics but it doesn't require some kind of decision to be made. Often this information is written down in a few sentences and added to the agenda in advance so people can read it before the meeting. This way, in the actual meeting you simply check whether the information was clear and if there is anything else to add or to ask."

I nod to show I understand.

"After that, you evaluate and, if necessary, evolve any previous agreements you've made that have reached the evaluation date," Bernie continues. "Here again, it's useful for everyone to look over these agreements beforehand, to check if they have any objections or concerns around them."

"I now see why it's really helpful to prepare for a governance meeting in advance," Carlos comments.

"Absolutely," Bernie nods.

I make a mental note to reflect on how we could prepare as efficiently as possible, wondering whether we could put everything into a shared document ahead of our meetings.

Meanwhile, Bernie is already moving on.

"Then it's time to address the prioritized governance drivers from the backlog. You take them one by one, recording all agreements you come to in the process. About 10 minutes before you planned to finish the meeting, you should briefly evaluate the governance meeting itself. It really helps to reflect on what worked well and what you could do to improve your practice for the next time. If you write these reflections down and read through them as part of your preparation for the next meeting, you'll remember what you've learned and avoid repeating mistakes again. After that evaluation, I usually ask for a few words from everyone about how they're doing now, prior to closing the meeting."

Governance meeting

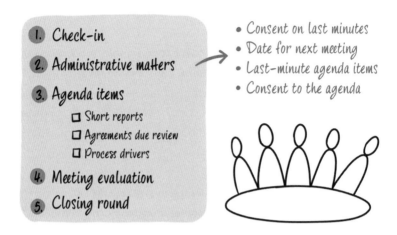

1. Check-in
2. Administrative matters
3. Agenda items
   - ☐ Short reports
   - ☐ Agreements due review
   - ☐ Process drivers
4. Meeting evaluation
5. Closing round

- Consent on last minutes
- Date for next meeting
- Last-minute agenda items
- Consent to the agenda

When there seem to be no more questions, Bernie suggests we take a short break and then spend the rest of the time we have together on the governance meeting tackling the governance drivers that are currently on our flip chart.

18

CONSENT DECISION MAKING

After the break, I walk back into the meeting room gingerly balancing my overly filled cup of coffee. Bernie has written something on the flip chart sheet in big beautiful letters and taped it on the wall. "Is my behavior in this moment the greatest contribution I can make to the effectiveness of this collaboration?" it says, under the header, "Artful Participation".

"This isn't so artful," I laugh, looking at Carlos as I clumsily try to place my cup on the table, spilling some of my coffee.

Artful participation

Is my behavior in this moment the greatest contribution I can make to the effectiveness of this collaboration?

"Artful Participation," Bernie announces solemnly when we're ready to start again. "For me, this is a very important pattern in S3. Not only because it's an essential ingredient in any successful collaboration, but because it's also an open invitation for self-reflection and personal development. The pattern invites you as an individual, and as a group, to collaborate as consciously and 'artfully' as possible."

Bernie points to the sheet.

"Reflecting regularly on your behavior gives you the opportunity to become more aware of your habits and assumptions, as well as your feelings and the needs behind them. Building self-awareness helps you to more consciously choose how to act in each moment. Within a team or organization, this enables you to participate and contribute more effectively."

Artful participation is an invitation for self-reflection and personal growth.

"And how does that work concretely?" Peter asks skeptically. "You can't just keep asking that question of one another. That would be a nuisance."

I realize from Peter's facial expression that the last sentence came out more emphatically than he'd intended. Bernie, as usual, stays calm and gives Peter a friendly smile.

"No, of course," Bernie says to Peter. "It's typically no fun to be asked that question, although it might be useful on some occasions if you're prepared to look at yourself in the mirror. But what's most powerful is to regularly ask yourself the question."

"Because," Bernie says, and again turns to the whole group, "we all have parts of ourselves that we prefer not to look at and try our best to hide, although they often slip through anyhow. And there are also other parts that we identify with strongly and that can take a lot of space. These are often strategies that we needed when we were children; they helped us to feel safe and to get our basic needs met. The thing is, as adults, different behaviors are sometimes more appropriate, but if we're running on autopilot it's easy to overlook that. The irony is that those habitual behaviors can bring about exactly what we're trying to avoid."

Bernie looks at us and asks: "Have you ever noticed that?"

We nod. Everyone is quiet and seems reflective.

"Asking yourself whether your behavior at any given moment is the greatest contribution to the effectiveness of your collaboration helps to create awareness, and awareness is a precursor to intentional change."

"It's also important to remember to be gentle with yourselves and with each other," Bernie continues. "Because judging yourself doesn't help much either, except to see what belief systems you're running on, of course. Instead, acceptance and compassion help to bring things into consciousness so you have the option to change if you wish. Artful participation is a simple yet very powerful tool for that."

"I'm sorry," Peter says softly.

"No need to apologize, Peter," Bernie says, smiling. "On the contrary, no doubt there was a piece of wisdom in your reaction. And perhaps you were afraid of something too. Anger often conceals a vulnerability about something."

Peter thinks for a moment.

"I don't have an answer right away."

He hesitates and then continues: "Maybe I'm afraid that we'll just end up talking about ourselves and our feelings, and this whole thing becomes nothing but a feel-good exercise when we should be concentrating on getting on with the actual work."

"You're completely right, Peter," Bernie answers. He laughs. "I'd get tired of that pretty quickly too! Sometimes it pays to bring a conversation to an end and focus on the agenda again. Sometimes participating artfully means saying nothing at all, while in other moments, it might mean speaking up and voicing an objection. You might even decide to break a previously made agreement from time to time when it makes sense to do so. Actually, S3 has a pattern for this, called breaking agreements. So, as you can see, artful participation is an invitation to put yourself in service of the most effective collaboration possible."

"So that means that it was actually pretty artful of you to get angry, Peter," Carlos quips.

We all laugh, and Peter relaxes too.

"Good," Bernie says. "Does anyone have an objection to experimenting with this pattern together? And are you ready to regularly remind yourselves and one another of this question?"

Everyone, including Peter, nods in agreement.

"Great," Bernie says. "So, let's get started with our governance meeting then."

He gets up and moves the three Post-its with our governance drivers from "To be decided" to "Agenda", and places them neatly according to priority, from top to bottom.

"Since we only have three drivers on our backlog, I propose that we put them all on the agenda for today's governance meeting," Bernie suggests. "Does anyone have any objections?"

We all shake our heads.

"Great," he responds. "Are there any short reports before we begin?"

Apparently there aren't. As we don't have any previously made agreements to evaluate either, we start with the first governance driver on the agenda, which came from Julia. It's about the amount of teleworking her HR team is authorized to do. It seems that my speech at the all-hands meeting generated quite a discussion in her team on the agreements around working from home. The current rule is that every employee, in consultation with his supervisor, can work from home one day per week on a fixed and agreed-upon day.

A number of people in the HR department say there are times when they can work much more effectively from home and they'd like to be able to do so. Julia is unsure how to deal with their request.

"On the one hand," she explains, "I'd love to give freedom and responsibility to my team members, but on the other hand, I'm worried about the continuity of work to be done."

"Let's check, just to be sure," Bernie asks. "Is this conversation a decision that belongs to our team? Or can Julia make these choices with her own team without having to talk to you about it?"

He looks around the table. Carlos and Sarah shrug.

"That's a difficult question," Peter sighs, more to himself than to us.

"I really wanted to discuss it with you," Julia says, "because I think that as the management team we should stand behind any changes regarding working from home, since other employees will learn about it and have questions for sure. So I'd at least like to hear your opinions."

Everyone nods.

"Then it's clearly a driver that needs to be considered first in this group," Bernie agrees.

"Should HRS employees be able to work from home more often? Does anyone have a proposal for this?" Bernie asks and waits patiently.

"Well," I begin, "what if we considered this as an experiment at HRS and asked them to come up with a solution that won't harm the organization, but instead would make it even stronger? That would be a great step toward more autonomy, wouldn't it?"

I look around and see mixed feelings among my colleagues. It looks like no one dares to respond to my idea.

"This seems to me a good opportunity to learn about consent decision making," Bernie says. He is clearly happy with the situation.

"Let's use the most elaborate form of the consent decision-making process," he suggests. "It's a very useful pattern in S3, and can help us to examine Chris's proposal in an effective way."

He looks around the circle and asks, "Does anyone have an objection to experimenting with consent decision making for the proposal that Chris just brought up?"

I chuckle when I realize that Bernie is seeking consent for using the consent decision-making process. He truly lives and breathes the S3 principles. Bart realizes it too, and smiles admiringly.

"Okay," Bernie says as he turns over a new sheet on the flip chart. "First, let me explain a few different ways that decisions are made. Firstly, there's autocratic decision making. That's when one person or a small group, usually the highest up the hierarchy, has the power to decide without taking anyone else into account. What are the advantages of that?"

"It leads to quick decisions," Carlos says, "which is quite the opposite of what we often do: look for consensus and deliberate without coming to any conclusion."

"Correct, Carlos," Bernie says. "And what are the disadvantages?"

"You don't necessarily make the best decision if you don't listen to the others," Sarah responds. "And people aren't involved."

"Correct," Bernie says. "You could also vote for a proposal and let the majority decide. What would be appealing in that?"

"More people would feel involved, but still not entirely," I say. "At least, it would be faster than looking for consensus."

Bernie nods. "Right. But what many people forget is that often the more creative and innovative ideas come from the minority first. Innovation is difficult and slow in a system where a majority is needed for each decision." Bernie looks around and continues.

"To use collective intelligence to the greatest extent possible, you actually want a type of decision making where everyone can be involved — without the snail's pace that often goes hand in hand with consensus. And that's exactly the purpose of consent.

You want a decision-making process that uses collective intelligence to the greatest extent possible.

In consent, everyone can have an influence on decision making, without necessarily getting directly involved in the process. Making decisions by consent means accepting a proposal as long as there is no valid objection."

"So, it's best to start with a concrete proposal. In S3 this proposal is either created by a group, or brought by an individual as in this case," Bernie continues. "Basically, you consider the proposal and adapt it to resolve any objections. It's often much faster than in a consensus decision-making process where you're constantly trying to weigh and adapt all ideas until everyone wholeheartedly says 'yes'. That can be really difficult, especially as often everyone wants to have their say, and you try to take into account all possible scenarios."

"Can any objection stop a proposal?" Bart asks. "Because then, just as with consensus, anyone could prevent a decision from being made. That doesn't seem very efficient to me."

"Good point, Bart," Bernie nods. "The big difference here is that an objection must be grounded in a solid reason why the proposal could lead to unintended consequences for the organization or how it could be improved in a worthwhile way. In consent decision making, the power shifts from a person to a reasoned argument. If someone cannot or is not willing to offer a reason that can be understood by the group, his argument doesn't qualify as an objection."

"Interesting," Bart says. "That's a significant difference between consent and consensus."

"Exactly," Bernie responds. "In consent, decisions are made based on the inherent wisdom that lives in the group but that isn't yet expressed in the proposal. Objections reveal wisdom that wants to see the light of day."

Consent

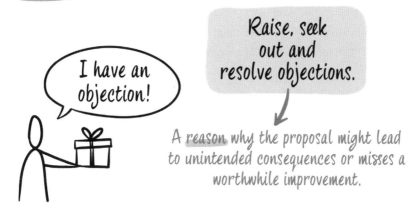

"Okay," Bernie says, looking at the clock. "Let's continue."

Bart, Peter and Sarah seem enthusiastic. Carlos and Julia still look a bit confused.

"The consent decision-making process in S3," Bernie explains, "consists of eight steps. The first one is called consent to driver. Because behind every proposal there's a driver and it's really helpful to be sure that everyone understands why the proposal is on the table in the first place. In our case, Julia was asked by her employees to have more autonomy with regard to working from home so they can work more effectively. At the same time,

Julia wants to ensure the continuity of the work to be done and to get full support from you as the management team."

"The questions we have to ask ourselves during this first step," Bernie continues, "are whether this driver is described clearly enough and if it's relevant for us to respond to it. What do you think?"

We all find the driver summary to be clear enough and relevant.

"Great," Bernie nods. "Then we have consent to the driver and can go on with the second step, which is to start from a concrete proposal. Chris, how did you formulate that again?"

"I propose to have the HR team come up with their own solution and to be sure whatever they decide has a positive benefit on their work and the organization as a whole," I answer.

"Okay," Bernie says. He asks me to write it on a flipchart and meanwhile continues: "The third step is to see whether anyone has any clarifying questions."

"Clarifying questions?" Sarah frowns.

"These are questions to understand the proposal as it's written. It's not a moment for getting into judgements or asking questions about why something is one way or another. That comes next."

"Then I have a question," Sarah nods. "Will Julia be involved in working out the solution in your proposal, Chris?"

"That's what I assumed, yes," I reply.

"And can the other departments decide on teleworking too?" Bart asks.

"Hmm, I don't really know. I haven't thought about that yet," I hesitate.

"That's quite alright, Chris," Bernie reassures me. "Bart, is it clear to you that this proposal doesn't include any suggestions relating to other departments?"

Bart nods.

"Good, then you understand the proposal as it is, and that's all we're looking for in this step. A proposal doesn't need to include answers to all possible questions, and if the proposal isn't yet good enough for now and safe enough to try, that will show up later through objections being raised."

Bart nods. No one seems to have any other questions about the proposal.

"Wonderful," Bernie says. "Then we can move on to the fourth step which is called brief response. This is a moment when everyone briefly shares something about their thoughts and feelings relating to the proposal. Not in detail, and certainly no discussion. But I would like to hear one or two words or sentences from each of you."

Bernie motions to Carlos to begin, and we share one by one.

"Happy," Carlos says. "I think this is a worthwhile experiment."

Julia, sitting to Carlos's left, says: "Good for me. And curious at the same time."

"I'm unsure," Peter says.

"Hmm," Bart says, frowning. "I see a lot of good stuff here."

"Super," Sarah says. "I think it's great that issues like working from home are up for discussion and that one team can go ahead and try something out."

"It feels totally fine for me," I say, completing the round.

"Great," Bernie says. "So, now we have a sense of your first thoughts and feelings about the proposal. It looks like it may be going in a good direction, but would still need some improvements to be good enough. Let's go to the fifth step — looking for objections."

"In this step, instead of using a round and going one by one, I'm going to invite you to all respond at once," Bernie explains. "This way, we preserve equivalence and avoid influencing one another's opinion. To help with this, I'm going to introduce you to some useful hand gestures we can use to find out whether you have any objections about this proposal or not."

"Okay," he continues, "Consider for yourselves whether you think this proposal is good enough for now and safe enough to go on with. If you think it is, you can show it this way."

Bernie stick up his thumb.

"You might see a reason why we shouldn't move forward with this proposal," Bernie continues. "Because you anticipate it might lead to unintended consequences for the organization or because you see what you think is a worthwhile way to improve the proposal. If so, this would indicate a possible objection, and we'd consider it before coming to any decision."

"You can show it like this," he explains, holding out an open hand, as if he was offering us something on his palm.

"Oh, I was expecting you to show us a thumbs down for a possible objection," Sarah comments.

"I deliberately don't do that," Bernie explains. "It could come across as negative, whereas every possible objection is a gift that you give to the group. A missing piece of wisdom that wants to emerge. Holding out an open hand is like offering that gift to the group."

This makes me laugh. Bernie really never does anything without a reason.

Every objection is a gift that you give to the group, as it contains wisdom that wants to emerge

"Alternatively," Bernie continues his explanation, "if you don't believe you have an objection to the proposal, but you're concerned, you can show your concern this way."

He holds his hand out horizontally, fingers spread, wobbling it a bit.

"Let's try it," Bernie says. "Like playing Rock Paper Scissors, we'll raise our hands when ready but we won't reveal our choice until after a count of three."

He repeats my proposal and we all hold out our arms with a closed fist. After Bernie counts to three, we show each other our choice. Everyone sticks up their thumb, except Peter and Julia. Julia indicates that she's concerned and Peter has a possible objection.

"This means that we won't move forward with the proposal just yet, because Peter may have a gift for us," Bernie says.

I admire the way he acknowledges Peter.

"At this moment, Peter has a possible objection," Bernie explains. "So, first we want to determine whether Peter's argument qualifies as an objection. Tell us, Peter."

"I'm worried about the reactions from other departments," Peter says. "If everyone can take a decision on the subject of working from home just like that, we'll end up in chaos. That's a recipe for disaster."

I react immediately: "Yes, but still I want everyone to take more autonomous decisions, to increase motivation and improve results."

"Well," Peter begins.

I don't let him finish: "We really need these kinds of experiments, Peter."
Bernie stops me in my tracks.

"Wait a minute please, Chris," he says calmly. "Step six in the consent deci-sion-making process is called Resolve Objections, which means integrating any wisdom revealed through objections into an amended and improved proposal. Let's first check to see if Peter's argument qualifies, and if so, we can aim for a both-and-more way to improve the proposal that combines Peter's wisdom with yours."

He turns to Peter. "So, you're worried about chaos and a potentially negative impact on the results, right?"

Peter nods.

"Okay," Bernie says, turning to us. "So, first of all, does everyone understand Peter's argument?"

We all nod.

"So, I want you to consider for a moment, does this argument qualify as an objection?"

He pauses while everyone considers his question.

"Does anyone disagree with Peter's argument, totally, or in part?" Bernie asks.

Again we think for a moment.

"I think you have a point," Bart finally says, turning to Peter.

Carlos and Julia signal that they do too.

Bernie looks at me.

"You don't have to agree with Peter, Chris, and if you disagree with him in some way then now is the time to say."

"I think he raises an important point," I say.

"Okay," Bernie nods. "So, what we've just done is to qualify Peter's argument as an objection."

He gives us a few seconds to let his words sink in before he goes on.

"Don't forget: any argument revealing why a proposal could lead to unin-tended consequences you'd rather avoid, or revealing worthwhile ways to improve the proposal, is considered an objection. Therefore, you really don't have to be afraid to speak up. The diversity of perspectives in the group helps you determine whether an argument is a valid objection or not, which in this instance appears to be the case."

Every argument revealing why a proposal could lead to unintended consequences, or revealing worthwhile ways it can be improved, is considered to be an objection.

"But what happens when someone cannot really explain his objection right away?" Sarah asks. "Often, I feel things intuitively, and I have trouble putting words to it to explain myself clearly."

"What would you do in such a case?" Bernie asks the group, his eyes twinkling. He clearly enjoys guiding us through this thinking process.

"Well," Carlos says, "in that case, perhaps we could help Sarah by asking her some questions?"

"Or you could give me a bit more time," Sarah adds. "Often what my feelings were telling me only occurs to me later on."

"Indeed," Bernie confirms. "Clarifying objections together can sometimes take some time. It also requires that a person raising a possible objection is willing to engage in self-reflection," he adds. "I think that's important. If someone voices a possible objection but then refuses to explain it or to examine it, it wouldn't yet qualify as an objection."

"Makes sense," Bart agrees.

When he sees our puzzled looks, Bart explains himself.

"Accountability, remember?" he says. "Equivalence goes hand in hand with transparency and taking responsibility. This means you can't just come with a possible objection without explaining it or being willing to self-reflect."

"Beautifully said, Bart," Julia nods.

Bernie nods in agreement.

"Are you ready to work with Peter's objection to see how we can resolve it?" he asks. "Because now that the objection has been qualified, we can try to integrate its wisdom into the proposal."

He looks at Peter.

Equivalence goes hand in hand with transparency and taking responsibility.

"How could I reformulate Chris's proposal to resolve your objection, Peter? What would you minimally need to adapt or add to this proposal to make it good enough and safe enough for now?"

"Hmm." Peter thinks for a while, and Bernie quietly gives him time to do so.

Peter finally speaks: "What if we asked the HR team to include a way to frequently evaluate their work-from-home experience, and any solution they come up with. This will allow them to measure whether it's detrimental to their results or to the rest of the organization. We then ask them to communicate this clearly to the other departments, both at the beginning of their experiment and at each evaluation."

Before we can respond, Bernie stops us: "I suggest we avoid losing time hearing everyone's opinion."

He winks at me and I blush.

"In principle, if we made this amendment to the proposal by adding frequent evaluation by the HR team and clear communication to the other departments, would anyone have any objections or concerns? I mean, only to this amendment of the proposal, not the proposal as a whole."

We all stick out our fists and, on Bernie's signal, show what we think about it. All thumbs are up.

"Great," Bernie says. "Could you write down the amendment and add it to our proposal?" he asks Peter, passing him the Post-it pad and pen.

Peter writes down his suggestion while Bernie continues: "Then let's zoom out and look at the whole proposal again, including the amendment: to let the HR department come up with a solution that has a positive benefit on their work and the organization as a whole, evaluating it frequently and communicating clearly. Does anyone see a reason why this proposal would lead to unintended consequences or misses a worthwhile way we can improve?"

All thumbs are up, except for Bart who's wobbling an open hand.

"What's that gesture about, Bart?" Sarah asks.

"Sorry. I don't know whether I have a concern or a possible objection," he says.

"When in doubt, it's always better to raise a possible objection," Bernie responds. "This way, we can help you discover whether your argument is an objection or not. It's perfectly okay to discover something is only a concern instead of an objection while trying to understand your reasoning. Sometimes explaining your argument to the group helps you discover there's no concern or objection at all."

"Okay," Bart responds, "then I think I might have an objection. We talked about evaluating and evolving agreements earlier on, and I really valued that. And while the proposal includes the HR team's evaluation of their approach, it doesn't include anything about us evaluating this agreement we're making about that. And I'm afraid we won't follow up on whether allowing them to come up with a solution themselves is actually working well enough or not."

"Oh, yes, you're right," Julia replies.

All the others are nodding too.

"So," Bernie says, "your spontaneous reactions indicate that you understand Bart's argument and that you see how it reveals that the current proposal isn't yet good enough. But I just want to check to be sure: do any of you disagree at all with this argument?"

Now we all shake our heads in unison.

"Meaning it qualifies as an objection," Bernie concludes. "Great. I'm glad you remembered the pattern about evaluating agreements and see the value of it. Now, how could we amend the proposal to resolve your objection, Bart?"

"It's as simple as adding a review frequency, I think," says Bart. "And I'd propose that in general we review this agreement three times a year, so every four months. But I'd also like us to initially evaluate it one month from now, so that we're all up to speed with how it's going and can tweak things if it's helpful."

Bernie seems to hesitate for a moment, but then says: "Okay, let's see. Are there any objections or concerns to this amendment, to add a review frequency of four months?"

All thumbs go up, except for Julia who's showing an open hand.

"You have a possible objection, Julia," Bernie says smiling. "Can you explain your argument to us, please?"

"Sure," Julia responds. "If we're adding an evaluation period for this agreement, we should also add evaluation criteria. That's what the pattern for evaluating and evolving agreements suggests, doesn't it?"

"It does," Bernie confirms. "But before going into that, I want to stick to the process of resolving objections. You didn't explain your argument, but instead immediately proposed an amendment to resolve your possible objection, namely to add evaluation criteria. Before going into the amendment itself: what might be unintended consequences of the current proposal if we don't add evaluation criteria? Or why do you think the proposal could be improved if we added them?"

"Oh, right," Julia responds. "Well, we didn't agree on what would determine the success of this agreement, except for what's indicated in the driver summary, of course. So I think we'll be able to evaluate it far more efficiently and effectively if we agree now on some evaluation criteria, and if we do it today while we're all fully connected to this topic and the underlying driver."

"Thanks," Bernie says. "So, does everyone understand Julia's argument?" We all nod and then he continues, "Okay, now consider whether this argument qualifies as an objection or not."

He allows us a moment to think about it before asking, "Does anyone disagree with this argument, totally or in part?"

We all shake our heads.

"Great," Bernie responds. "So, it qualifies. Do you see how we first qualified the objection, before getting into actually amending the proposal. And how we're using the group's combined intelligence to do so?"

We all nod again. I'm glad Bernie is being so meticulous in the way he's helping us to learn the process. It seems it could be easy to skip or confuse some of the steps until we understand the process well.

"Julia, could you now repeat what you proposed as an amendment to the amendment?"

"The what?" Sarah asks, seeking eye contact with us to check whether we understood Bernie's phrasing.

"I had an objection," Bart explains to Sarah, "and proposed to amend the proposal by adding an evaluation frequency. Julia had an objection to that, and now she's proposing to add evaluation criteria, which is an amendment resolving her objection to the amendment I had proposed to resolve mine."

"Ah, right," Sarah says. "Now I understand."

"Me too," says Carlos. "Resolving objections requires you to be very attentive to where you are in the process, apparently."

"It does," Bernie confirms. "Thanks for explaining so well, Bart. Now, Julia, what was your amendment?"

"To spend a few moments, immediately after reaching this agreement, on adding a couple of evaluation criteria," she responds.

"Okay," Bernie says. "Let's check for objections to this amendment first. Any objections or concerns to what Julia just said?"

All thumbs go up simultaneously. We're getting used to this ritual.

"Then let's zoom out again to the whole proposal," Bernie guides us, "including the amendment made by Bart and Julia to add a four month review frequency and list some evaluation criteria right after finishing this consent decision-making process. Any objections or concerns to the whole proposal?"

Again, all thumbs are up. Even Julia's initial concern seems to have vanished. I'm impressed by the effectiveness of this approach.

"Congratulations," Bernie says. "You've just reached an agreement. So, we can celebrate having come to a decision, one that is good enough for now and safe enough to try."

Consent Decision Making

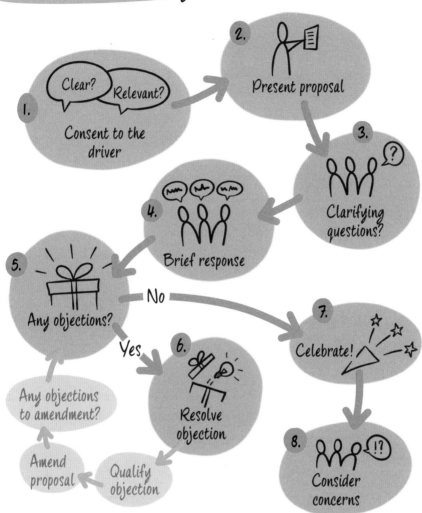

1. Consent to the driver — Clear? Relevant?
2. Present proposal
3. Clarifying questions?
4. Brief response
5. Any objections? — No / Yes
6. Resolve objection — Qualify objection — Amend proposal — Any objections to amendment?
7. Celebrate!
8. Consider concerns

Bernie gets up and gives us all a high-five. It feels a bit unnatural, but I understand that he wants to explicitly show and celebrate that all objections have been resolved and that the proposal has therefore become an agreement.

"Wow," Sarah says. "This really works."

"Indeed," I agree. "Sorry for my defensive reaction earlier on, Peter," I say. "I'm glad Bernie stopped me."

"It was actually the process that stopped you, Chris," Bernie says smiling. "It invited us to check for any wisdom behind Peter's argument. It pays to trust the process."

Everyone nods enthusiastically.

"What would have happened if Julia or anyone else had still had a concern?" I ask.

"Well, we'd have still celebrated coming to an agreement first," Bernie says, "because a concern doesn't stop a proposal from becoming an agreement. Only objections do that. Then I'd have asked Bart if he thought it was worthwhile for us to hear about his concern right now, or not. If yes, then we'd listen, and maybe even tweak the agreement to mitigate his concern. If not, I'd have asked him to at least record his concern, alongside any evaluation criteria we'd already recorded, in the agreement. This way we'd acknowledge his concern and we'd check it again when evaluating this agreement, at the latest, in case it turns out to be more than just a concern."

It's sensible to at least understand the concerns and record them as evaluation criteria.

"Great, that sounds like a logical thing to do," I respond.

"Indeed," Bernie says. "Confusing concerns with objections and trying to resolve them as an objection can quickly lead you away from consent decision making and back toward trying to reach consensus. So be cautious about that."

We spend the next five minutes agreeing on some evaluation criteria for the agreement. For that, Bernie uses a round again, asking us one by one to propose evaluation criteria, each time checking for possible objections before moving on. This way, we end up with a list of five acceptance criteria.

"Super," Julia sighs when we're finished. "My team will be happy with this agreement. This afternoon, we have our team meeting and I can immediately put them to work on deciding how to proceed with this."

"Hmm," Bernie thinks out loud. "That's perhaps a good opportunity to introduce another important S3 pattern too."

"Tell us," Julia encourages him.

"Well, Co-Create Proposals is an S3 pattern that helps people to co-create a proposal as a response to a driver. This way, they tap the collective intelligence, build a sense of ownership and increase the level of engagement."

"We could certainly use that," Carlos chuckles. "How does it work?"

"Well, you can co-create proposals in many ways. S3 includes one specific pattern for that, called Proposal Forming, but the easiest way to learn about it is through actually using it to respond to a driver."

We look at our governance backlog but none of the most important drivers has any immediate need for a proposal or the co-creation of one. So we decide to stick to our priorities and to learn about proposal forming at a later date, when it's helping us to respond to an actual driver.

Bernie offers to help Julia and her team to use proposal forming this afternoon when they consider the driver about working from home. I'm so curious about this pattern that I ask whether I could come to observe. Neither Julia nor Bernie has a problem with that, as long as the HR team has no objections.

We continue and respond to another two drivers on the backlog. The first one is about the way Peter will collect information for press releases. For the second one, which is a proposal Bart brought about modifying the license of one of our business intelligence tools, we practice consent decision making once more. This again shows us the power of the consent decision-making process, resolving all objections one by one until the proposal is good enough and safe enough.

"Good," Bernie says, looking at his watch. "We still have more than 10 minutes left before the meeting is officially over, but I'd like to stop working on our governance backlog and introduce another S3 pattern called Evaluate Meetings."

"It's very valuable," he continues, "to briefly evaluate each meeting, to reflect on our experience so we can improve for next time. And, to leave adequate time to formally close together too, before people head off to whatever they're going to do next."

It's important to briefly evaluate each meeting.

Bernie starts the meeting evaluation and asks us to first share some thoughts of appreciation about our meeting. He invites us to go around the circle using rounds, a pattern that we know well by now. Julia begins and shares her enthusiasm about the way we learned about consent decision making through doing. She also appreciates the autonomy we gave her HR team while retaining some co-ownership as the management team. Sarah explains how happy she is to have learned the distinction between governance and operations. She expects that this governance meeting approach and its conscious facilitation will help us a lot.

We finish the round hearing from each in turn. Everyone experienced the morning as very positive, and I'm happy about their enthusiasm. And about the results of this new approach. Not only did our meeting go more smoothly and with greater focus than our usual Monday morning sessions, the atmosphere was quite different too. Granted, Paul and Steve are no longer with us, and I have a different role at the table, but I'm convinced that these are not the main reasons for the change. Applying S3 and the gentle but clear guidance by Bernie are already beginning to bear fruit.

After the round of appreciations, Bernie asks whether we now have any suggestions about ways we can improve our meetings, to run them even more effectively in future. He asks Carlos to begin the round and to go the other way around.

Carlos passes. "I have no idea how this can be improved," he laughs.

"I have something," I say when it's my turn. "Bernie taught us that a governance meeting needs to be prepared by at least bringing the governance backlog up to date."

I look at Bernie for confirmation. He nods.

"How are we going to do that?" I ask. "Where will we manage our backlogs, because I suspect that leaving these flip chart sheets here on the wall isn't the best option. We'll have no walls left before long. Does anyone have an objection to the idea of making some kind of shared spreadsheet and ensuring that we record any drivers that come up for the following meeting? Maybe it's also useful to include details about what we think is actually needed to respond to a particular driver and about any preparation that would be useful?"

No one has an objection.

"Good," I say. "Then I'll set it up and send you a reminder on Friday morning to look at everything for our Monday meeting."

"Great," Bernie laughs. "Then you're our first logbook keeper."

When he sees my confused look, he explains: "Logbook Keeper is a pattern in S3 too. The key responsibility of this role is basically to document all information and agreements required for collaboration in the Logbook. Which could be any kind of document or system that fits this purpose."

"This role doesn't always have to be formally defined," he adds. "For us, what you just proposed seems good enough."

I nod.

"Okay," Bernie continues our round. "Any other important improvement suggestions?"

There are none, apparently, so Bernie goes on.

"So as a way to close, I'd like to invite you to turn your attention inwards by making contact with your bodies and your breathing."

We shift around on our chairs a bit, and I close my eyes. That helps.

"Feel into how you are right now, at the end of this meeting, and whether there's anything that needs attention or wants to be said. You may do that very briefly now and, rather than using rounds, just speak if you feel moved to do so."

Bernie lets the silence have its effect, until Julia hesitantly begins.

"I'm leaving this meeting very happy," she says.

We nod.

"This was very interesting," Peter adds."

"Thank you, Bernie," Carlos says. "I learned a lot today."

We all nod again.

A long pause, and then Sarah says with a smile: "I'm hungry."

We laugh.

"Perfect," Bernie says. "Let's go for lunch. Enjoy your meal!"

Before we leave the room, I encourage my colleagues once again to urge their people to come to the driver mapping workshop on Wednesday. And I promise myself to do the same with Steve tomorrow in a one-to-one conversation.

19

BERNIE'S OPINION

"What do you think?" I ask Bernie as we walk to the cafeteria for lunch after the meeting. He takes his time before answering.

"On one hand, I'm impressed," he begins hesitantly. "It's beautiful to see how quickly everyone, except Steve, of course, follows this new way of thinking. That's really not to be taken for granted, or underestimated."

I nod.

"Still, it's too bad that Steve doesn't want to be part of it," I sigh.

"I don't think so at all," Bernie says.

I look at Bernie in surprise.

"It would be a lot easier if he had joined us from the start," I explain.

"I don't know, Chris," Bernie says.

He stops walking and looks at me.

"Every objection contains a chunk of wisdom, and so does Steve's refusal to participate. It would have been a lot more difficult if he'd not dared to refuse and had joined us instead, just for appearances. At least he's being honest, and you know what you can or cannot expect of him."

We continue walking. Bernie's comment makes me think of Peter. Is he really being honest? Sometimes I have this nagging feeling that Peter is not always upfront.

Before I can ask Bernie what he thinks of Peter, he picks up the conversation again: "Don't forget that Steve, by his decision, is living proof that you as the CEO mean what you say, namely that you're striving for equivalence, and intend to use your hierarchical powers as little as possible. The fact that you let Steve choose his own pace and approach is a very strong signal to the entire organization."

That's something I hadn't taken into consideration. On the contrary, I thought it was rather weak of me as the CEO to not have been able to get the whole management team on board.

"Thank you, Bernie," I say sincerely. "I'd never looked at it this way before. But go on, I interrupted you with my comments about Steve."

You will have to unlearn at least as many habits as you need to learn new things.

"Like I said, I saw that you, as the management team, have made some great strides over the last two Mondays. And at the same time, I have begun to understand how much more difficult it will be to implement S3 in your company than at The Facts."

"What do you mean?" I ask.

"At The Facts, we decided to use S3 from the very start, which meant that we were able to build everything up along S3 principles as we let our company grow. We've hired people that fit that culture. You've already been in business for some years now, and you already have processes, structures and a culture that everyone at HRS is used to. This means that you'll have to unlearn at least as many habits as you need to learn new things. And this will require a lot of time and attention."

I nod. I'd already realized that.

"How long do you think it might take us?"

"I've no idea, Chris," Bernie replies. "I'm just as curious as you as to how this will all unfold."

Bernie puts his arms around my shoulders and laughs. "Don't worry too much!"

20

PROPOSAL FORMING

"No, for me that doesn't feel right," Elena says cautiously.

Bernie had just explained the concept of a driver to Julia's HR team, and Elena clearly doesn't agree with her colleague Rick's first attempt to summarize a driver about working from home. He'd just suggested unlimited teleworking for everyone, for the "what's needed" part of the driver summary.

"Interesting," Bernie says, smiling at Elena. "Tell us."

"For me, it's not just about how much or how often we work from home," she explains. "I simply want more freedom to decide when I want to work from home. As it is now, I have to work from home every Friday, but that means that I sometimes miss important events here at HRS, and occasionally it would be better for my family if I could work from home on a Monday or Wednesday."

Some of her colleagues nod. They clearly agree with Elena's comment.

"Yes, me too," Juan adds. "There are busy periods or special occasions when I would prefer to work here on a Monday rather than from home. As it is now, I'm scheduled to work from home on Mondays, even if it negatively affects some meetings or discussions."

"Thank you, Juan," Bernie says.

"And how would you improve or add to Rick's description of what's happening and needed?" he asks Elena.

"Could you repeat the first part?" Elena asks.

"Okay," Bernie says. "At this time, everyone works from home for a maximum of one day, on a fixed day?"

"Hmm," Elena says while thinking for a moment. "Perhaps I would like to add something about the problems that this sometimes creates."

Some of her colleagues nod. So does Rick.

"What do you think about the following?" Elena asks her colleagues. "Currently, everyone works from home for a maximum of one day, on a fixed day. This leads to unnecessary inefficiency, for instance. people miss important meetings or are not able to focus."

Everyone seems happy with this summary of what is happening.

"Great," Bernie says, again looking at Elena. "And what's needed for this group?"

Elena looks around, seeking eye contact with the others. She frowns, thinks for a bit and finally says, "How does this sound? We need greater flexibility on how often and when we'll work from home, to allow us to work better together and further improve our work-life balance."

She looks around the circle. It appears that people agree and some are even smiling happily.

"Super," says one woman with short hair whose name I don't know. Rick raises his thumb.

I'm somewhat surprised — positively so. I had thought their issue was to be able to work from home more often. But it looks like the group is also concerned about better collaboration, which is sometimes hampered by working from home. For that reason alone, I'm happy that no one from the HR team had an objection to me observing the meeting.

Julia looks at me; she obviously thinks the same.

"Beautiful," Bernie says. He writes the driver summary that Elena just formulated at the top of a blank sheet.

"Is this summary clear enough for everyone?" Bernie asks.

Everyone seems to agree.

"Great. This was the first, important step in co-creating a proposal using the proposal forming pattern," he explains. "You just established consent to the driver, which means that it's described clearly enough and you consider it relevant to respond to it. By the way, it's often useful to have any conversations needed to ensure a driver is described clearly enough before you all meet face-to-face, so you don't lose unnecessary time during the meeting itself."

While taking notes, I realize that we usually skip this step, which means that we often work on issues that are not entirely clear to everyone, or we spend a great deal of our meeting discussing and sometimes arguing about what the issue actually is, or working on things that are not that important.

"So, the next step is called questions about the driver," Bernie continues. "You've already asked some questions about the driver, to be able to summarize it clearly enough. But it's possible that you have further questions about what's been happening and is needed, which will help in figuring out how to respond to this driver effectively."

It's useful to have any necessary conversations to describe a driver clearly enough prior to meeting.

"Could we perhaps set up a monthly planning tool about working from home?" Juan asks.

Before everyone jumps to an answer, Bernie steps in: "That's a great question, Juan. It seems to me your question reveals a possible solution, right?" Juan nods.

"That's useful information," Bernie continues, "but right now we're still in the step of checking for any more questions to understand the driver itself. So we're still focusing on the past and the present, not yet on the future. So could you write down your idea and we'll come back to it later in the process?"

"Sure," Juan responds.

"I do have a question about the driver," Julia says. "Which misunderstandings and slow-downs are we talking about? May I hear some examples?"

The group provides plenty of examples, for instance how working from home sometimes requires people to call in to important meetings and how that slows down the conversations. Or how during busy periods, some colleagues have trouble concentrating in the office and would much rather spend a few days working from home to focus better.

"Great," Bernie says when Julia shows that she's heard enough. "Any more questions about the driver?"

There are no more questions, so Bernie announces that it is now time to look ahead and start working toward possible solutions. The objective is to collect as much wisdom and input from the whole group as possible, and to then take those findings into a smaller subgroup that will craft a concrete proposal.

"Before we get into hearing actual ideas, the first thing we'll do," Bernie explains, "is to think about and write down any considerations that are on your mind, regarding possible solutions. I'd like to ask you to express these considerations as questions. One kind of question we're looking for is questions you have about any constraints on what is possible. These are information gathering questions and they typically have only one right answer. The other type of question invites us to consider different options. We call these generative questions because they have many possible answers so they open up our thinking to come up with creative ideas later on.

Bernie gives us a few minutes to reflect individually and to write down our questions on Post-it notes. Then he asks us to share our questions in a round, one by one, sticking our Post-its onto a flip chart sheet as we go.

Hamza goes first. "Are there legal limitations on the amount of time people may work from home?"

"Yes," Julia responds, but before she can continue, Bernie interrupts: "Good question, Hamza. Let's look for the answers later and collect all the questions first."

He draws two columns on the flip chart, labels the left one "Information Gathering" and sticks Hamza's Post-it note in there.

"This seems to be an information gathering question," Bernie explains, "as it's a question for which there is only one possible answer. These kind of questions help us to understand any constraints on how you could respond to the driver."

Elena is next. "How much advance notice is required by the team when someone will be working from home?"

"What type of question is this?" Bernie asks.

"It's generative, I think," Elena replies.

"Indeed it is," Bernie confirms. "Because more than one answer is possible, and it's inviting us to reflect on solutions."

He sticks the Post-it on the flip chart paper, this time in the other column and labels it "Generative Questions".

"I also have one," Rick says. "Can't we put in our calendars when we work from home and make it visible to everyone?"

"This seems to me to be a third kind of question that's similar to the one Juan asked earlier," Bernie says smiling. "It sounds like a solution disguised as a question, don't you think?"

"Well, actually yes," Rick admits, blushing.

"Not a problem, Rick," Bernie reassures him. "Because it high-lights a potentially useful aspect of a solution. But for now, if you zoom out a bit, what generative question could you formulate around this?"

Reformulate solutions in disguise as neutral, generative questions.

Ricks thinks for a moment then says, "How can we ensure transparency and clarity about who works from home and when?"

"Sounds great," Bernie says and asks Rick to put this question on a Post-it note and stick it on the sheet.

"What are the risks that our team and HRS could face if we change the way we work from home?" Julia asks as she gives Bernie her Post-it.

"How can we meet the expectations of the management team in whatever we decide?" Juan adds, referring to the beginning of the meeting, when Julia had explained that we as the management team want the organization to be positively affected by any changes to the ways people work from home.

"Do we need to have someone physically present at all times?" Tina reads out loud.

Bernie posts all the questions in the appropriate column on the flip chart until no one has anything left to add. I look at my watch and realize that this whole exercise took us only seven or eight minutes. There's a lot of interest-ing questions, many of which I'd never have thought about myself.

Bernie then asks us all to gather around the flip chart and to answer what-ever informative questions we can. This is how we discover, for example, which concrete legal limits exist around working from home.

After having written the answers onto the Post-its, Bernie asks us to quick-ly prioritize all the generative questions. He suggests we sort the Post-its in silence, put the most important at the top, and put aside any disputed cards until all the others are sorted.

Thirty seconds later that's done, with the exception of two that Elena and Juan had tried to put in different places. A brief conversation between the two of them reveals where to place these questions too and in a little over a minute we're done. Bernie explains that this is useful for those who'll later put the proposal together, as they can then take these priorities into consideration.

Bernie concludes this part of the process, prepares a new flip chart sheet and hands out more Post-its.

"Now, finally, we're going to collect ideas," he explains. "To do so, let's once again spend a few minutes first, to reflect individually. What concrete ideas do you have about how to respond to the driver? You might for example have an idea about a solution to the entire driver or various ideas which address elements of the solution or of one or several of the prioritized considerations. Write down one idea per Post-it, keep your writing legible and summarized using only a few words. Afterwards we'll stick them all up on this flip chart, but keep them to yourselves for now, okay?"

Everyone gets to work. It's so quiet you could hear a pin drop. Some write down only one or two ideas, others seem to have a lot of inspiration.

After a few minutes, Bernie breaks the silence, asking everyone to finish up. He invites us to each read out an idea in turn using rounds and tells us to only read out the words we've written down. He reassures us that this is not a time for asking questions unless an idea is unclear. And he teaches us a useful trick: if someone shares the same or a similar idea to one we have written down, then we can say "bingo" and only explain any extra details, to cover all the points while avoiding duplicating Post-its on our board.

With Elena's help, Bernie places each idea on the board in turn and very soon we are looking at a variety of ideas and suggestions.

Proposal Forming

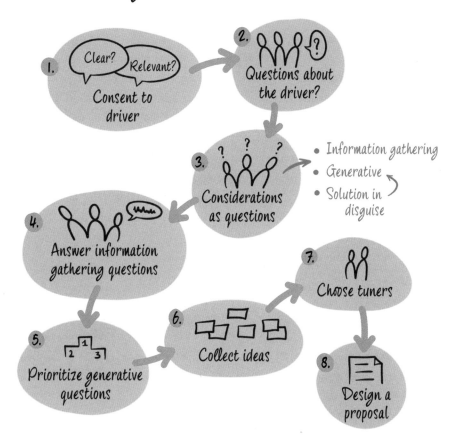

"Up until now, the purpose of this exercise has been to gather and share knowledge, thoughts, and ideas and compile it all on these two flip chart sheets. As you can see, we've gathered a lot in a short space of time," Bernie notes, "which will help us in the next step — to create an actual proposal, based on this information."

"However," Bernie continues, "trying to build the proposal with everyone would be inefficient. That's why I'd suggest that a smaller group of at least two, and no more than three people, take all this information with them to create a proposal for us, and bring it to the next meeting. We call this little group the 'tuners', and they'll be responsible for tuning the proposal in a way that they think effectively responds to the driver. They'll do this using the wisdom harnessed in the considerations and ideas you've gathered. Just as tuning a piano brings the strings in harmony with one another."

He pauses to let his words sink in and then continues: "They can of course call on other people to help if they consider that valuable. Afterwards, the tuners will present the proposal and we'll use the consent decision-making process to check for objections and concerns. There, you might discover that the proposal needs to be improved. But by having done this preparatory work together first, there's a good chance that the proposal may already be good enough, or that it requires only a few objections to be resolved before it is."

"Typically, the group chooses the tuners," Bernie explains. "It is important to timebox that conversation and usually two or three minutes are enough. What we're looking for is anyone from this group who should be involved, anyone who wants to be, and anyone else who would be worthwhile to include. So, any suggestions?"

Hamza says: "I would like to see Rick and Julia tune a proposal. Rick, because of his passion for the subject, and Julia, because as our manager, she'll have to endorse the proposal anyway, and because she knows the organization better than we do."

"Great, thank you, Hamza," Bernie says.

"So we have a proposal," Bernie explains to the group. "Let's see whether anyone has an objection to Julia and Rick being the tuners for this proposal? Or concerns?"

"Yes, I do," Julia responds. "Thanks very much for your trust, Hamza, but I would prefer not to work on the proposal, because I don't want to influence it too much — consciously or unconsciously — in my role and position as manager. I deliberately wanted to give you all the autonomy to do it."

I'm happy about Julia's response. This sends a clear signal toward her team. "Thank you, Julia," Bernie says. "Does anyone disagree that Julia's argument qualifies as an objection?"

Nobody does, although a few look appreciatively toward Julia.

"Who else other than Julia should be tuning this proposal?" he asks the group? "Who could significantly contribute alongside Rick?"

"Could I propose myself?" Hamza asks. "I'd like to work on this topic, and I think I have a pretty good sense of the wider organization too."

"Of course, you could," Bernie says. "Does anyone have an objection to Rick and Hamza being the tuners for this proposal?"

There are no objections. I look at my watch and again realize how quickly this went. We've been working on this proposal forming exercise for only half an hour, even though this group has never worked with this process before. I'm impressed.

Bernie then explains to us what a proposal needs to look like. A good proposal contains the original driver and the description of the proposed response to this driver. It also includes who will be accountable for what. And, because it's important to evaluate to what extent the implementation of the proposal is an effective response to the driver, evaluation criteria and an evaluation date have to be added too.

Proposal

Bernie reminds us of the importance of empiricism and continuous improvement and reassures Hamza and Rick that they don't need to spend too much time on constructing the proposal.

"We're looking for a proposal that's good enough for now and safe enough to try," he explains. "So, there's no need to try to work out all the possible details or scenarios. When you present the proposal to the group to check for consent, any objections people raise will reveal pieces of wisdom that you may have overlooked."

Hamza and Rick show they understand, and we agree that they'll present the proposal during the next team meeting next Monday. Bernie offers to be present again.

"And if you want," he says, "I'll teach you the consent decision-making process next week, in other words, how to come to an agreement based on Rick and Hamza's proposal."

"That sounds great," Hamza says. "I've really enjoyed using proposal forming today. If we can learn even more, I'm up for it."

The rest of the group is also very enthusiastic about the idea. I appreciate the modular aspect of S3 more and more. Bernie isn't imposing anything on anyone but simply introducing patterns that can help to address concrete needs as they arise. It works really well.

"Shouldn't we also invite the management team to this next meeting?" Elena interrupts my thoughts.

She looks at Julia and myself: "After all, you'll have to approve our proposal, won't you?"

I'm not sure what to say and look at Julia. Her expression tells me that she doesn't have a clear answer either.

"I don't really know," I finally say honestly. "On the one hand, I would love to be there to participate in the process and to learn from it. But on the other hand, I don't want to interfere with it. I really find it fantastic that you'll work out something yourselves. And for the management team and me, it's enough if Julia supports the experiment that you will engage in. She's perfectly capable to represent the entire management team concerning this."

"Wouldn't you still want to be there?" Elena asks as she looks around the room for support. "If only to fully understand our proposal and our experiment."

"Just in case other departments ask questions about it," she adds when she sees my doubtful look. "I'm a bit worried about that."

The others nod, and I finally agree to come and participate.

"Great," says Bernie, who'd been keeping out of this last conversation. "So we'll see one another again next week. And don't hesitate to ask me for help if you get stuck in constructing your proposal," he says to Rick and Hamza.

Bernie and I say goodbye to the HR team and walk over to the cafeteria for a cup of coffee. He also seems to be happy with the exercise and trusts that Hamza and Rick will come up with a good proposal.

21

STEVE

The next work day begins with my first weekly one-to-one conversation with Steve. I'm not looking forward to it, but I understand it's important to remain on good terms with him. I intend to always keep his positive intentions in mind, even if we have different approaches and opinions about a number of things. Bernie emphasized this again yesterday and helped me to understand that the organization can learn a lot from Steve's resistance to S3.

The weather is nice, so I suggest to Steve that we walk around the block instead of meeting in the office. The minute we step outside he begins talking. "We're starting to have a problem in my department, Chris. Up until this week, we spent a lot of time on version 4.0 and we're now in the process of solving the very last issues around it. We should be able to finally deliver by the end of the week. But after that, my people could start finding themselves without work because there's no planning for version 5.0 yet, nor any clarity on our clients' expectations."

I make eye contact with Steve and encourage him to continue.

"I've already talked to Sarah about it," he says. "Because it's her people who usually take care of the new requirements, but lately they've been too busy trying to sell version 4.0 and smooth out issues with getting it delivered. They still have to find out what's required for version 5.0."

He stops and looks at me.

"This is a real problem, Chris. Starting from next week or shortly after, my people will no longer have any valuable work to do."

"Hmm," I sigh. "I'm glad you're telling me Steve. This is indeed not good news, I suppose."

We remain silent while we continue walking. I'm trying to sort out my thoughts.

"Would you tell me a bit more about the situation?" I continue. "How much longer exactly can your people be meaningfully engaged in their current work? And what could they start doing for version 5.0?"

Steve explains that there are still a few minor adjustments required for version 4.0 that they've agreed with clients, and that this will keep his teams busy for another two or three weeks after the official release. But not everyone will be involved in this, which means that as of next week, some of his people will be without work. A few of them are worried and are asking questions about it, others are taking a wait-and-see attitude. Steve goes on to say that some of his architects are already making technical plans for version 5.0 without knowing the exact functional requirements. This is risky, but Steve doesn't know what other kind of work he can give them.

"I really must have a concrete and detailed plan for version 5.0 so that my people can get to work," he concludes.

I feel resistance rising within me against his need to have a preconceived, detailed plan. There isn't one, and there won't be one for a while. On the other hand, he does have a point. We don't know how to start with 5.0, however critical it is for the survival of HRS. And soon there will be people without work.

"You're right," I say sincerely, looking at him. He seems surprised by my comment. "We need to take action around version 5.0 as quickly as possible. It will indeed be a problem if your people are without work for too long."

I hesitate and stop walking.

"Steve, at the same time, I want to be clear, and I need to ask you a difficult question. There won't be a detailed plan or analysis for 5.0 like we had for earlier versions. We'll no longer be setting everything in stone in great detail, only to find out a year later that our clients weren't happy with our choices. That was the case with version 4.0, with all its dire consequences. You know as well as I do that HRS cannot allow itself another release like that."

He nods, but seeing his frown and the shrug of his shoulders, I realize that he's not happy to hear that. And the most difficult part is yet to come.

"I want to ask you to invite your people to work on version 5.0 in a different way, namely together with Sales and Marketing and with the teams that make the mobile software. The tough part is that we'll have to learn what that new way of working is as we go along. And we will start tomorrow."

"What do you mean?" he asks.

"Have you heard about the driver mapping workshop that we scheduled for tomorrow?" I ask.

Steve nods.

"Yes, I've heard about it," he says.

I explain to Steve the purpose of the workshop.

"I'd love it if a few of your people could be at this workshop to bring the concerns and needs of your team into the mix," I say. "My hope is to get a picture of the most important drivers we need to consider in the new HRS. A successful version 5.0 is a crucial element in this."

I pause for a while before I go on. My words seem to have landed with Steve.

"For me, the real work with version 5.0 starts tomorrow," I continue. "You and at least a few of your people have some legitimate questions about it. It would be a real shame if we couldn't include your needs, ideas and energy in our efforts."

I put my hand on his shoulder and look at him.

"I really mean it, Steve. I understand that we're two very different people, each one of us with our strengths and shortcomings. But let's go beyond our differences and find ways of working together based on our shared concern for HRS and our product. We'll need you and your people tomorrow to get version 5.0 on track."

"I already told you that I'm not going to participate in your S3 stuff," he says grumpily.

He continues walking without looking at me. I suppress my urge to try to convince him and remain silent. It's Steve who finally breaks the silence.

"I really appreciate that you take my concerns seriously," he says, now more softly. "And I also know that you, just like me, want only the best for HRS."

"Great," I sigh. "That's right. So, you'll be there tomorrow?"

Steve laughs and shakes his head.

"You are a tough one, Chris. I want to be part of building our company and our software, but I can't promise anything for tomorrow."

"Okay, fair enough," I say. "But could you please not prevent people from your teams joining us tomorrow if they would want to?"

Again, Steve pauses for a long time before he answers: "Okay, I won't keep anyone from coming. I'll even personally tell this to my teams today so that it's clear for them as well."

"Thank you, Steve," I say, relieved. I'm really hoping that some of Steve's group will show up tomorrow. Otherwise, we'll have a huge problem.

22

A MORE AGILE AND EFFECTIVE HRS

It's Wednesday morning, and I'm in the office at 7.30am. The driver mapping workshop won't start until 9am but I want to make sure that our meeting room is well set up. As instructed by Bernie, I get us a number of flip charts and plenty of markers and Post-it notes. I create space for a large circle of chairs in the middle of the room and put several tables in the corners to allow for work in small groups. I clean the whiteboard and prepare some sheets on the flip charts. On each of these sheets, I draw a circle, with an empty governance board on one side, and an operations board on the other. The circles represent domains, which will hopefully be created later this morning.

Finally, I place a vase with flowers and some treats in the middle of the circle of chairs.

"Hi, Chris," Bernie laughs as he walks into the room. "You're up bright and early. Not too nervous?"

"Well, yes, a bit," I answer. "It feels like the real change only starts today."

"Indeed, today we'll begin to co-create a new HRS," says Bernie. "And it's going to give us a first idea about what it can look like. I'm just as curious as you are."

"I only hope that we'll have enough people show up today," I sigh. "I'm really tense; it feels like my baptism of fire as the new CEO, although I won't be doing much today. The ideas will have to come from the people themselves."

"Don't worry, Chris," Bernie smiles. "It's going to be all right."

He looks around the room and nods approvingly.

"Nice. We only need one more sheet with the primary driver for today written up on it. The one you showed at the all-hands meeting. Why don't you go ahead and prepare that before we start? Your handwriting is so much better than mine."

I write up the driver and hang it on the wall above the whiteboard to make our common goal visible to everyone. Meanwhile it's 8.30am and I still have time for a cup of coffee before everyone arrives.

A good half an hour later, 38 people are in the room. We even had to add a few chairs. I'm really happy with how many people have come, especially since there are representatives from all HRS departments. Steve is unfortunately not here, but I'm counting at least 14 people from his department, which is great.

After having thanked everyone for joining this session, I tell them again why we're here. I'm pointing at the sheet above the whiteboard, with our driver written on it in large letters: *"Due to the current structure and culture at HRS, we're confronted by a number of problems such as demotivation, slow decision making and ineffective collaboration between teams. This has prevented us from launching version 4.0 successfully, and puts HRS at risk. We need to become more agile and effective as an organization, so that we can create and deliver awesome products again in the near future."*

I emphasize again how much I believe in self-organization and equivalence before Bernie continues. He asks the participants to get in touch with their feet and their breathing. When it is completely quiet in the room, he asks the people to one by one summarize in literally one word how they feel this morning. A quick check-in round. It goes really well, and I realize once again how even a short round like this positively changes the atmosphere in the room.

"This is an important and exciting moment for me," I announce honestly after the check in. "Exciting, because I'm not here as the CEO or as a manager to tell you what to do, but with the intention of learning together with you what's needed to bring HRS back on track."

Again, I point to the driver above the whiteboard.

"This is a first exercise in self-organization," I continue. "Bernie will accompany us in discovering step by step what we'll need to create a more agile and effective HRS."

I pause deliberately and look around the circle before going on.

"You're here because you've chosen to be, and not because you have to. This applies to the whole session. If you feel at some point this morning that you're no longer learning or contributing anything, look for another spot in the room where you can, or feel free to leave if that's your preference. For me, this represents an essential element of invitation-based change, instead of a plan-driven change."

"Great," Bernie continues. "Let's begin. Today, we'll be using driver mapping to kickstart the necessary change at HRS. Driver mapping is an S3 pattern that will help you to collectively identify and organize drivers you'll need to respond to, to achieve our common goal. It helps you to create an initial organizational structure that supports this to the greatest extent possible, and to ensure that you can quickly begin working on the right things."

> **DEFINITIE**
>
> In a complex situation, driver mapping helps
> a group to identify and organize important drivers,
> and get to work responding to them in an appropriate
> organizational structure.

"I suggest that we start right away and learn by doing. So, I'll explain each step as we go," Bernie says. "Does anyone have an objection to that approach?"

Nobody seems to have an objection, so Bernie continues: "Okay, the first step is to come to an agreement about why we're here in the first place — our primary driver for needing to change things at HRS."

Bernie explains to the group what a driver is and how it can be properly summarized. He also explains how, according to S3, an organization shapes itself around actual drivers instead of around a fixed power hierarchy, and how this creates a network of interrelated drivers. He uses the flip chart to visualize his story.

"Later on in the workshop," he continues, "we'll cluster these drivers into coherent domains of work and consider how best to account for them with teams and perhaps some roles as well. But I'll explain this in greater detail later."

He points to the flip chart on the wall and says: "Let's first agree on why we're here. To do so, we want to introduce this driver to you: 'Making HRS more agile and effective and building awesome products again'."

"Is this driver summarized clearly enough for you?" Bernie asks. "And is it relevant enough for us to work on? If you don't think so, let us know."

Joe, an architect in Steve's team, raises his hand.

"Not really an objection," he says, "but a question. Could we also specifically talk about the next version of our product today? I really think it's important, because from a technical point of view, we'll have to tackle this very differently than the previous versions."

"Good question," Bernie answers. "If you think that a different technical approach of version 5.0 is needed to help make HRS more agile and effective, then you absolutely have to bring that in and work on it."

"Also from a functional perspective, our next version will have to be better," another person pipes up.

"Yes, and faster than the previous one. We really can't wait nine months this time," someone else adds.

Several people in the circle nod. Obviously, everyone has fully understood the importance of our next release.

Bernie takes the floor again: "I'm happy with all this energy. That's exactly what we need. Let's progressively collect all your good ideas. But before that, I'd like to conclude this first step and to ask again if anyone has an objection to this driver as our common goal for today? Is it sufficiently clear and relevant?"

No reactions.

"Great," Bernie says. "This means that we've achieved consent about the driver for this session. The next step is to explore which actors will be impacted in this endeavor. When I say actors I mean the individuals or groups of people who are involved or affected by us responding to our driver."

Bernie invites us to come up and stand around the blank whiteboard and asks us a number of questions: "Who can help us to deliver a great version of our product next time and help us make HRS overall more effective and agile? Who might prevent us from doing so? Who could benefit from us doing so and who could be harmed by this endeavor?"

Bernie gives us a minute to think. Then he asks us to take turns to name actors we have in mind. He'd already spread a number of large Post-its across the whiteboard and as each person suggests another, he invites them to come up and write the name of the actor on one. We end up with 15 in total. They include the users of our product, HRS employees, our competitors. The HRS employees are split up into management team, project leaders, technical architects, sales people, the HR department and all other employees.

"Good," Bernie says when we're done. "Time for the next step. Now I want to see what all these actors concretely need in relation to our driver, or what we need from them to make HRS more agile and effective."

He asks us to reflect individually on what we think is needed to respond to our primary driver, considering each actor. He suggests that we can think about it in terms of what we need, or need to do. Or in terms of what the actors need. He also asks that we include a brief explanation of what we think the impact of responding to that need would be. Each need and the anticipated impact of responding to it is written on a separate, light blue Post-it, with the name of the actor in the upper left-hand corner and the initials of the person writing the note in the upper right-hand corner. They are then placed next to the corresponding actor on the board. Bernie also tells us to leave a little space at the bottom of each Post-it for what will come next.

After less than 20 minutes, an impressive selection of what we consider to be important needs has appeared on the whiteboard. As everyone stands around the board, I have a look at what has been put there. I see, among other things, that the management team needs to grant more freedom; that the technical architects need more insight into what our clients really want; and that our clients want significantly smaller and more frequent updates of the product.

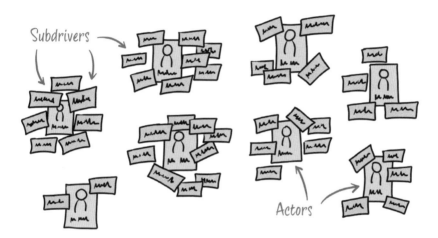

Bernie purposely doesn't give us time to read all the Post-its and is already moving on.

"Super," he says. "On this board we now have a number of suggestions about things needed, grouped around the actors. In fact, all the light blue Post-its are suggested subdrivers of our primary driver. By responding to these subdrivers we are also responding to our primary driver."

"But these are not yet all of the possible subdrivers, are they?" someone asks.

"No, indeed," Bernie replies. "But there is a good chance that we have re-vealed and recorded many important ones. Part of the purpose of this ex-ercise is to bring out as much wisdom as possible from the group in a short time."

"And think about it," he continues, "if we have overlooked an important need at this stage, would that be a problem?"

A long pause, until someone suggests: "Couldn't we simply add it?"

"Exactly," Bernie nods. "That's what Chris referred to in the all-hands meeting when he spoke about a living system and getting away from planning everything in detail. We want to become more agile, which means that we need to learn to work with what appears to be most valuable and effective at any given moment and then learn and adapt as we go."

Bernie checks whether there are any other questions or concerns. Given that there aren't, he explains the next step in the exercise.

"In this next step, I'd like to ask you to take some time to look over the various needs that people have written down. If you come across any subdriver that you have had some experience responding to in the past, or have ideas about, please add your name to the bottom of the Post-it. This way, whoever deals with it later knows they can call on you if they're looking for extra input. I'm sure you have some ideas on how we could tackle some of these needs, don't you?"

People nod.

He gives the group 15 minutes and sets up a timer. It takes a while before everyone gets into action. Some people wait and see, while others hesitantly approach the board. A few minutes later, everyone is in action. People help each other understand the various needs, or subdrivers, as Bernie pointed out, so that the right names end up on the right Post-it notes. When the timer goes off, Bernie asks everyone to finish up. I notice how nearly every subdriver has one or more names or initials written on it. Bernie thanks everyone for a job well done and announces a short break before continuing.

After the break, Bernie asks us to gather around the whiteboard again. Our next task is to reorganize all subdrivers and also the actors into meaningful clusters or groups. Duplicates are removed, and items that relate to each other are grouped together in a logical manner. He reassures us that there is no need for the subdrivers to stay with their original actors, since the name of the actor is written on each subdriver.

He also suggests that we reflect on how value is created in the organization and consider how we can group the various actors and subdrivers in a way that supports people to create or provide value end-to-end, as independently as possible. He points out that this clustering may not correspond to how the teams and departments in our organization are currently set up.

"Sometimes this step can get a bit chaotic," he warns us. "However, I trust your ability to organize yourselves. It's okay if not everyone is actively involved in the forefront, but we're aiming for a grouping of actors and needs that each of you supports. So, you'll have to talk to each other and make sure you understand what's on the board."

"To keep focus," Bernie continues, "I suggest that you work in two short iterations of seven minutes each. Take a brief moment for planning at the start and after the first seven minutes we'll quickly review what you've achieved, followed by a short retrospective to reflect on what went well and what you could do to improve your collaboration in the next iteration."

The timer is set and before long, a group of participants mingle in front of the board. Others are less active or simply observe. Meanwhile, Bernie and I distribute the sheets with the templates I had prepared earlier on the tables around the room, so they are ready for the next step.

Seven minutes later, the various subdrivers and actors have been organized into a number of groups on the board, some including actors, some without. There are also a few single subdrivers, which do not seem to have found a clear place in the big picture yet.

"So," Bernie says after he gets up to stand by the board. "Is it done yet?"

There's not much reaction, apart from some murmuring.

"Let's check whether we have consent on the groupings," Bernie says, smiling. "Consent means that you see no reason why continuing with the current clustering would lead to unintended consequences you'd rather avoid. It also means that you see no obvious and worthwhile way to improve this for now."

Bernie briefly explains the hand gestures and asks everyone to indicate whether they have any objections or concerns about what is currently displayed on the board. A lot of thumbs go up, but I also count at least eight possible objections as well as a number of concerns.

"I don't understand the grouping as it is on the board," someone who was objecting says. Several people nod.

"I do," someone else says, "but I'd like to see the loose drivers also be part of a group."

Bernie listens to the other arguments too, and suggests that we integrate the wisdom revealed through them in the next iteration. Before we start the clustering again, he invites everyone to reflect for a couple of minutes on how we're working together. Firstly, we comment on what we think is going well, and then people share some improvement suggestions. Finally, Bernie sets the timer again to seven minutes and takes a step back.

We decide that someone should explain the current groupings. Some people spontaneously take charge and in no time, everyone understands how the Post-it groups relate to one another. In the process, two more Post-it groups are added and a large one is split up. As a result, most of the loose drivers have found their place in an existing group. In total, we now have six driver groups, which means six domains.

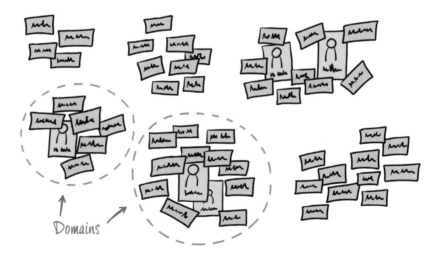

Domains

As the timer goes off, the group still needs a few seconds to finish up. Again, Bernie checks for objections to the current groupings on the board. This time, all thumbs go up.

I'm impressed by the process and by Bernie's facilitation, as minimalistic as it is at times. And again, the power of consent is evident, even in as large a group as this.

"Thank you all," Bernie says. "This looks very good."

"What you now see on the board," he explains, "are various groups of inter-related drivers. Each of the groups constitutes a domain. And each domain represents a specific area of activity, influence and decision making within the organization. In this case, the Post-it groups all represent subdomains within the larger, all-encompassing domain of the primary driver that we started our exercise with — the driver about the change toward a more agile and effective HRS that makes awesome products again."

Bernie had tried to explain this to me earlier, but it is only now that I fully understand the purpose and the power of driver mapping. Yesterday, the change required at HRS seemed terribly big and vague to me, and I had no idea how to begin. And now I have in front of me some clear, manageable subdomains with a lot of information about what is needed and who can help to meet these needs. I'm excited to get to work.

"Let's get back to work," Bernie says, smiling. "Can you come up to the board again, please? I'd like to ask you to feel into which of the domains you're attracted to, based on your current knowledge and experience. And your passions, talents or interests, of course."

"Which of these domains would you like to get involved with?" he asks after a brief pause. "At least for the rest of this workshop and hopefully longer. This way, we start out with a few people who have a certain expertise in each domain."

Bernie puts us to work. Groups form around the various domains and we take Post-its down from the wall to the tables where the templates that I prepared earlier are laid out. Bernie asks each group to investigate and talk through the various drivers summarized on the light blue Post-its, to understand what their particular domain is all about. Next, he invites us all to think of a name for our domain and summarize the driver that encompasses the various subdrivers that are on the sheet in front of us. He explains that this overarching driver is called the primary driver of the domain.

After some minutes, Bernie invites us to pause and each of our groups in turn shares briefly what we've come up with so far.

Next, he asks us to think about what essential subdrivers would need to be taken care of, to ensure that the primary driver for our particular domain is responded to effectively. To answer this question, he recommends selecting the most important subdrivers from the light blue Post-its and to add any drivers that might be missing but are important overall. This is how the participants are gradually building the first version of our domain descriptions. I notice that now and then people walk from one table to another. They're discovering that their domains overlap more than they'd initially thought. After some reflection with Bernie and the other groups, two groups decide to combine their domains into one.

"A nice example of how an agile organization constantly adapts to what's actually needed," Bernie says with a wink at me.

Once key responsibilities have been listed, Bernie asks us to think briefly through what constraints there might be on our particular domain, if any. And whether certain resources would be necessary to respond effectively. Finally we consider whether there are specific qualities, skills and experience that would be preferable for people to have when they account for our domain over time.

When all domain descriptions are almost done, Bernie invites us back into the circle of chairs in the middle of the room. He pulls in a flip chart and explains how teams and roles are commonly used in organizations as a way to account for domains. He talks about the properties of a circle, being a self-governing team, and how we could now create a circle or role to account for each domain on our whiteboard. Unless an agreement or a one-time action is enough to take care of a particular group of needs, of course. He points out that the sum of roles, circles and other types of teams, and the relationships between them, together define an organizational structure.

Bernie also explains about a commonly used pattern for building organizations that helps decision making across domains. When there are strong interdependencies between domains, teams select representatives, whose job is to represent the interests of one domain in another by participating in the other domain's decision making. This is called linking, or double linking, if representatives are selected both ways.

From my conversations with Bernie, I know that there are several other organizational structure patterns in S3. But he limits his explanation today to the most commonly used patterns to avoid overloading us with new information.

When he's done explaining, Bernie invites us to go back to our tables and consider what we think would be the best way to get started within our domains. He suggests that for now we could consider either a role or a circle. It soon becomes clear that all domains require a circle, because they all require the collaboration of several people to account for them. So we end up with five circles.

Bernie explains that circles are semi-autonomous. The members of a circle typically organize their own work and they govern themselves within the constraints of their domain, by means of regular governance meetings.

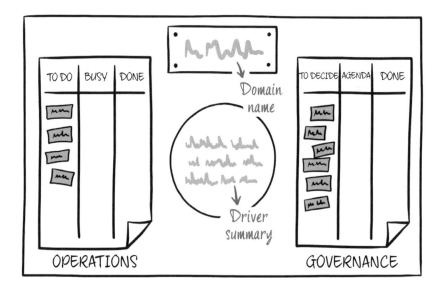

After having clarified the difference between governance and operations, Bernie asks us all to stick the light blue Post-its with the various drivers for our domain into the appropriate backlog on the template. The Post-its with a driver requiring a decision that will govern future decisions and activity are governance drivers and belong to the governance backlog; all other drivers belong to the operations backlog.

We go back to work. Bernie walks back and forth to help, because it is not always clear in which backlog a driver needs to go. Some of us discover that certain drivers don't fit into our domain. Bernie encourages us to take these drivers to the right table, to the domain in which they belong.

I notice how Bernie and a few of the participants collect drivers on a new, blank sheet. Just as I'm about to ask what's going on, Bernie interrupts the exercise and asks everyone to come back to the big circle of chairs for a minute. He places the sheet with the drivers he just collected in the center of the circle.

"Kathy, would you like to explain what just happened and why these drivers are here?" Bernie asks when everyone is seated.

"Well," Kathy explains, "in our domain there were a few governance drivers we could never decide on alone, because they impact several other domains that were created here today. That's why, with Bernie's help, we put them up separately here."

"We also have one of those," someone calls out.

"Then put it up on this flip chart as well," Bernie says. "Because when you have several circles working together around one big driver, it's normal that certain decisions will impact them all. A circle is supposed to work as autonomously as possible, but in practice, there is often quite a bit of overlap between domains. And there are dependencies too, so it's valuable to make some decisions together."

DEFINITION

In a delegate circle, representatives decide together how to respond to governance drivers that have an impact on several domains.

When he sees that the group has understood, he continues.

"You could hire a manager or coordinator to solve these issues across all circles, but in S3 the most typical solution is to create a Delegate Circle."

"A what?" Joe asks.

"A delegate circle."

"And how does that work?" I ask.

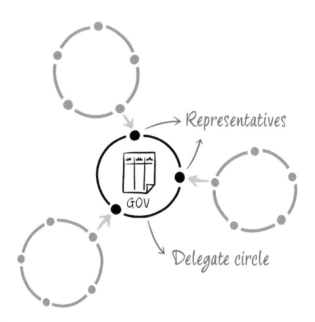

"Well, every circle that's affected, selects a representative. These representatives together form a new team, called the delegate circle. Together they make decisions about how to respond to drivers that concern the various teams involved, or where the result of a decision will impact all domains. Usually, a delegate circle holds regular governance meetings to address these common challenges, but they only do governance. Decisions made are acted on by the various teams themselves."

Bernie answers a few more questions and then invites everyone to go back to their domains and templates and to make sure that all drivers end up in the appropriate backlog. He puts up the sheet with the drivers for the delegate circle so that everyone can easily add drivers, if needed.

Ten minutes later, all groups seem to be about done. Bernie thanks everyone for their hard work and asks them to come back to the larger circle.

"So, you've identified a number of drivers and distributed them throughout five domains," Bernie summarizes. "You've decided, for now, to respond to each domain with a circle, and currently each of you is a member of one of those and has already begun responding to your domain's primary driver. The members of each circle can self-organize both the 'what' and the 'how' of their work, within the constraints of their domain. And overall governance of the system will be handled by your delegate circle, with decisions made there being acted on in your various circles."

He looks around the circle and continues: "What we have then is an emergent organizational structure that's evolving organically around the various drivers you've identified. This structure is good enough for now and safe enough to get started with. But it's not fixed or static. It can and will continue to develop and transform over time, as new drivers arise and you decide how to respond to them."

Timo, a specialist in online marketing from Sarah's team, interrupts Bernie: "How exactly does this work then? I'd like to learn a lot more about S3; it seems to be really useful for our job."

The organizational structure is not fixed or static. It will develop and transform over time, as new drivers arise and you decide how to respond to them.

"That's exactly what our circle is planning to do," Bianca, an analyst from Steve's department, responds. She points to the template of the domain that she was involved in.

"We gathered all drivers around self-organization and S3 in our circle, including training and coaching," Bianca explains.

"And you just proved the usefulness of this domain," Bernie smiles. "Would it be all right to park your question for the moment?" he asks Timo. Timo nods.

"Okay," Bernie continues. "Let's have a look at all the domains that have been created to give everyone here an overview."

One by one, the domain descriptions are explained by those who created them. Questions and comments from the group help to fine-tune them further.

Four of the circles are specifically focused on creating a successful version 5.0 of our product, with each circle approaching it from a different angle. The circle "Frequent Delivery" deals with regular and small releases of product increments instead of one big bang delivery. This will require, among other things, more automated testing and the automation of installations.

The second domain concerns the technical foundations of our product, which have to be improved and become more flexible. The somewhat cumbersome architecture of our product should be redesigned and include smaller, more independent components. This circle is named "Architecture". I'm really glad that these two circles were created today, because I have been trying to convince Steve for a long time — so far in vain — to invest in test automation and architecture, just as we did in our mobile department. I'm grateful that today this initiative has come from the people themselves. And that there were quite a few from Steve's team who worked on this domain.

In addition, there's a circle on involving our clients at an earlier stage and on more deeply understanding their real needs for version 5.0 — the circle "Happy Customers". The last of the four circles is about finding new clients for version 5.0 and selling our new product. This circle has the rather predictable name "Sales 5.0".

The fifth circle, the domain Bianca talked about, doesn't seem to be limited to version 5.0. It deals with improving overall collaboration, motivation and effectiveness at HRS. And, more concretely, with improving decision making, self-organization and collaboration, and learning how to apply S3 patterns. They've called it "Better Collaboration".

While the five domains are being explained, Bernie draws an overview of these new circles on the whiteboard.

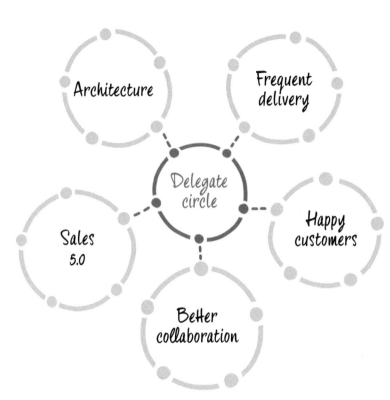

I'm impressed that, in just under three hours, we've not only learned a lot about driver mapping and numerous other patterns, but we've also come up with a concrete structure for the needed change — with plenty of motivated people who are ready to get to work on it.

As if Bernie had read my thoughts, he continues: "You have just created five new and important circles. That's no small feat."
I raise both thumbs to show how happy I am with it.
"Let's have a look at the next steps from here and then wrap up the session," Bernie says.

The first thing that needs to happen is to identify the members of the new circles. Bernie asks those who would like to join a circle and dedicate time to it to put their names on the template after the session.

He is also looking for one candidate per circle to take responsibility for getting things started. That means bringing the members together and organizing the first governance meeting — to then define a high level strategy with the circle members for how to go about responding to their driver. Each of these new teams will already have a lot of information at its disposal: the domain description; the subdrivers on the light blue Post-its; and the initials of colleagues who have concrete ideas for how to respond to them, if they need extra help.

Bernie explains that, in theory, each circle's strategy should be presented as a proposal, to their delegator, to check for any objections or concerns before going ahead. The delegator is a person or group that holds overall accountability for a domain but delegates responsibility for it to another person or group.

DEFINITION

The delegator is the person or group delegating responsibility for a domain to another person or group.

"In this case," Bernie explains, "responsibility has been delegated by the management team who is overall accountable for the driver we've been working on today."

Bernie pauses and seeks eye contact with me. I nod to indicate I agree. A quick glance at my colleagues from the management team shows me that they also think this is a good approach. The only person I can't see right away is Peter.

"Weird," I think, because he was still around just before the break. But I have no time to dwell on it, because Bernie is already continuing.

"I'd like you to understand that this structure is only good enough for now," he says. "A few days down the road you might well need something else. So when you start working in these circles, pay attention to tension you experience and look beyond it to see if there is an organizational driver that needs attention. There are many ways to respond to drivers but sometimes you discover the best approach is to make changes to the structure itself."

It will be quite difficult to keep track of the circles and their agreements if they keep on changing and evolving, I think. Perhaps I should explore whether a tool is available for this. But before I can ponder this further, there's a question from the group.

"Will all the new circles have leaders?" asks a woman whose name I don't know. I think she is from Peter's financial department. "Or do we have to completely self-organize ourselves within our domain?"

"Good question," Bernie says. "That depends on how the circle was created. Generally, the person or group who creates a new domain — the delegator — determines the domain's boundaries and constraints. Usually, a delegator lets members of a new domain decide for themselves how to organize their work. But if and when it makes sense, they may insist that a specific role gets installed. For example, a coordinator."

Paying attention to tension will show us the most effective structure at any given moment.

Bernie looks at me again and goes on.

"In your case, the management team is the delegator and they are giving you the responsibility and freedom to choose the best possible strategy, which means that you decide yourselves whether your domain needs formal, leading roles or not. But understand that this really is not always necessary."

Bernie looks expectantly at me, so I step in: "Personally, I'd like to see as much self-organization in your circles as possible. This will require attention and possibly some guidance and coaching in the beginning too. But it's a powerful way of working together, and nature shows us plenty of examples, by the way."

"And at the same time," I continue, "sometimes self-organization is simply not the most effective way of working. So a circle could quite rightly install a coordinating role, or select someone into a role to prioritize the work for the circle. I'd suggest, use your common sense."

Self-organization doesn't happen by itself. It requires a common goal and clear boundaries.

"And remember," Bernie continues, "to submit your strategy as a proposal to the management team as soon as it's ready. By making it a shared agreement, they will actively share accountability for the outcomes too."

I nod to show I fully agree with Bernie.

"Perhaps I should emphasize," I say, "that self-organization doesn't happen by itself. I learned that lesson when we started working on the mobile software with self-organizing teams. We discovered that we needed a common goal and clear boundaries. S3 helps by inviting you to clarify what the driver is for any collaboration and define domains clearly with a domain description. But that's not enough, because you also have to change behavioral and thinking patterns that might have been around for years. And this requires practice and discipline and often some kind of guide or coach, or someone with experience in self-organization who can help."

"You just formulated a nice driver," Bernie smiles. "The need for support for self-organizing teams."

"No worries," Bianca responds, while pointing to the template for the "Better Collaboration" domain. "That driver was already on our backlog."

Bernie continues and explains briefly how each circle can organize their drivers and their work by visualizing work in governance and operations boards. He offers to facilitate the first governance meeting of each circle to support everyone in learning about S3 as we go along.

In wrapping up, I thank everyone for their commitment in this session, and emphasize how happy I am with this step in our process. I ask them to inform their colleagues about this session and the new circles, and to invite them to join a circle if they wish to contribute.

We end the workshop with a check-in round where everyone briefly shares how they feel about all of this now. Although there's still some confusion and doubt, especially about concrete ways to move forward, the reactions are overall quite positive and hopeful. I don't seem to be the only one who'll leave this session with a lot of energy and trust.

———

After almost everyone has left the room, I add my name to the circle "Better Collaboration". I really want to contribute to this domain. Bernie also writes his name on that template.

I hesitate for a minute, pondering whether I should join the "Architecture" circle too. I still enjoy working on the technical and architectural aspects of our software. But I decide not to add my name. I worry that people from Steve's department might see me as the CEO who wants to meddle with coding, which is the last thing I want. There are enough technical experts in the organization, and I secretly hope that Steve will become involved with this circle.

Even though he and I are completely different in terms of management style and personality, Steve is a darn good architect who knows our systems through and through. If he'd support the circles we just created, he'd be able to contribute a great deal content-wise. This might fill the void that's likely to arise as his people gradually organize themselves and he discovers that he no longer needs to be leading their daily planning and operations.

23

It bothers me all afternoon that Peter left the driver mapping workshop early. Perhaps he had a good reason, but my instinct tells me to be careful. Which is why I haven't yet talked to him directly.

On my way home, I decide to call Paul. I share my concern with him and ask him what he thinks about Peter's reactions to the changes.

"In a way, your question is justified, Chris," Paul answers. "Peter is the only one I was a bit concerned about before I announced my resignation at the board. In the past, he's made no secret of his aspiration to take over as CEO one day. Given his role as financial director and member of the board, this seemed logical. But I don't believe that he can bring in the new wind that HRS needs. That's why I asked you instead."

"And how did he react to this news?" I ask Paul.

"Well," Paul answers, "Peter's first reaction was not so positive. I don't think he immediately understood why I thought you were more suitable. But when I once again explained the problems HRS was going to face and that our current way of thinking wouldn't solve them, he began to come around. The fact that all the other board members reacted positively right away might have helped too. Peter was the only one who initially showed reservations about you as my successor."

I start to feel uncomfortable. I'm glad I was unaware of this when I took up the job, because I might not have had the courage to do so.

When my end of the line falls quiet, Paul continues: "Don't worry, Chris. By the end of the board meeting, Peter was completely convinced. He seemed to fully understand why I had chosen you and said that he'd support you in your mission, as did all the other board members too."

"And that seems to be the case," I have to admit.

"Just give him some time. He still needs to get used to it," Paul reassures me.

"I hope so," I answer. But my gut feeling tells me to remain alert about Peter.

"Something else," Paul continues. "We've been able to solve all the problems with the release and I think that version 4.0 can be rolled out this weekend."

"Super, that is great news," I say.

"You'd think so," I hear Paul sigh. "Today, two of our big clients told us that they're no longer interested in this version. For one, because we're so late with our delivery and it no longer fits into their planning, but mainly because during testing they discovered a few important new functionalities in our software that are unsatisfactory."

"Oh, technical problems?" I ask.

"No, in the end everything works. But we don't seem to have understood some of their genuine requirements at the beginning of the release. To be honest, we did get some heads-up about it earlier, but we didn't think that they wouldn't buy the new version."

I feel myself getting angry. I so often pleaded for faster, smaller-scale releases enabling us to get more frequent feedback from customers, but I was never able to convince the management team.

"I know, Chris," says Paul, who is guessing my thoughts. "And that's why I have stepped aside to leave it up to you. This is yet another sign that HRS really has to change its approach."

"Okay," I say. "What does this mean for us?"

"Many smaller clients and our other big clients do want to roll out this version, so that's good. But we'll have less revenue from this release than expected. And we need to restore trust with our clients. I'm more convinced than ever that the next version of our product will be crucial for the future of HRS."

I swallow involuntarily.

24

PETER'S BLUNDER

The energy I'd derived from the driver mapping session is brutally crushed to bits the following morning. When I get up the next day, I have eight missed phone calls and one sms from Paul: "Serious problem here. Come as fast as you can."

I skip my shower and breakfast and rush to HRS. On the way there, I listen to voicemail messages from Paul and Julia. It appears that this morning, an interview with Peter was published on an influential HR website in which he and HRS were portrayed extremely negatively. Mainly because Peter was unable to explain the upcoming changes at HRS.

"We have to fix this issue as quickly as possible," were the last words of Paul's voicemail message.

"I should have taken on the role of spokesperson myself," I sigh as I stop the car at a red light. I'm angry. About Peter, but perhaps also about myself. Maybe I should have been more cautious, because nominating people for a role and then giving them so much autonomy doesn't seem to work. Paul would never have given up this responsibility.

I'm still talking angrily to myself as I arrive at HRS. Julia, Sarah and Paul are waiting for me and begin to talk over one another to tell me what's happened. I don't understand a thing, so I'm happy when Sarah hands me a printout of the interview. I plop into a chair and begin to read.

The interview starts out all right, but very quickly the conversation turns to our new approach. Peter talks about self-organization and suggests that there is no longer any structure or leadership at HRS and that everyone can do whatever he wants. Peter seems to be easy prey for the interviewer, who asks tough and leading questions. Peter clearly doesn't know how to take a stance and constantly contradicts himself. The interviewer closes the interview with the words: "I hope there will be someone at HRS who can bring the company back on track, because the way it seems to be going, I fear the worst for its clients and shareholders."

"Phew," I sigh. "It won't be long before the stock market reacts to this, and not in a good way."

I look at the others in resignation. Paul is the only one who seems to be holding a glimmer of hope.

"Chin up," he says. "Losing a battle doesn't mean you lost the war."

"You're not angry?" I ask incredulously.

"No," Paul says firmly. "I've known Peter long enough to be sure that he didn't do this on purpose. It's not good for his personal reputation either, you know. First, I'd like to understand what happened and then think about a plan for how to fix it."

Right at that moment, Peter walks into the meeting room looking gloomy. He's obviously aware of what happened. He's agitated as he explains how the interviewer had promised to give him the article to review and correct before publishing, but that he didn't get that opportunity. And now the interview appeared unexpectedly this morning. He's genuinely shaken by what happened, which appeases my anger and makes me take a calmer look at the situation.

"It's okay, Peter," I reassure him. "We know you had no bad intentions."

Paul nods and looks at me. He's clearly glad that I was able to calm down.

"Let's have a look at the facts," I suggest. Peter grabs a chair and Sarah gets coffee.

We discover that Peter was indeed caught by surprise by the journalist's questions during the interview. He'd expected questions about the products and finances of HRS and was not properly prepared to talk about the changes and S3, which got him into trouble and which the interviewer gladly took advantage of. Moreover, Peter never received the chance to read the interview prior to publication, as had been promised.

"But why didn't you tell us about this earlier, Peter?" Julia asks. "Didn't you do this interview on Monday?"

"Yes," Peter hesitates. "But I didn't dare to admit that I'd blundered so much and thought that by reviewing the text, I could put it right."

I'm surprised by how little Peter has understood S3 and the way we want to work but I decide not to bring it up for now.

"It is what it is," I say. "Let's see how we can resolve this together."

I look around the circle, hoping for help or ideas. After some reflection, we decide to demand that the journalist grant us a new interview to rectify the story. Sarah will take care of that; she's good at this type of negotiation. Paul and I will prepare and give this new interview together. And after explaining everything to them, Paul and I will ask the board members to confirm their trust in our approach in public.

"We also need to say something to our clients," Sarah comments. "I just saw in my emails that we have already received concerned phone calls from two clients triggered by the interview."

"Let's take this as an opportunity to approach our biggest clients personally and explain our ideas to them," Julia suggests.

"Yes," I answer enthusiastically. "And let's include one or two people from the new "Happy Customers" circle in those conversations. That's exactly what they wanted: to work more closely with our clients, and this gives them the chance to introduce themselves. Who knows, this situation might just bring us closer to some of our customers."

I'm glad that the atmosphere has become more positive and that we have a plan to act on.

"What can I do?" Peter asks. "I feel terribly guilty about all this."

"Come with me to see the journalist," Sarah proposes. "Together, we'll be able to win him over, I'm sure."

"And I'd like to understand how this could have happened, Peter," Paul says cautiously. "Is there something missing in your knowledge or understanding about self-organization or S3? Or do the principles run so strongly against your own internal beliefs and needs that you can't present a good story? Because the latter would have been the case for me, which is why I asked Chris to pull this forward. I wouldn't have been able to do that."

Peter wants to reply, but Paul stops him with a gentle hand gesture.

"No need to answer right now, Peter. Simply think about it yourself."

"And don't worry about the article," I say sincerely. "No hard feelings. We all make mistakes. Let's just try to learn from this case."

"Thank you," Peter says, clearly relieved that he did not get a major reprimand.

25

DINING OUT WITH KATE

It's Friday evening and I've taken Kate out for dinner and a movie. It's been such an intense week at HRS, and I'm happy that the weekend has arrived. Although work-related, it could become an exciting weekend. The latest tests of version 4.0 were positive, and so Paul and some HRS colleagues will bring the new version into production this evening and tomorrow, enabling the clients who signed up for version 4.0 to start working with it on Monday. I offered to come along, but Paul refused. He assured me that everything would be fine, and that I should focus solely on version 5.0 and the future. But I do plan to keep my mobile phone nearby this weekend. You never know. On the way to the restaurant I tell Kate how Peter's interview seems to have turned out positively in the end. Sarah and Peter arranged a second article about HRS to straighten out the situation. And the board sent some positive signals into the world after a conversation with Paul and me. But what I'm most excited about is a visit to one of our big clients. The management there had been concerned by the article, and so Sarah and some people from the "Happy Customers" circle went to talk to them.

After having reassured the senior management of that client, they stayed on for several hours afterwards to speak to some important end users of our product. This is how they learned why version 4.0 failed to be a success, but above all what the users expect in version 5.0.

As a result of that conversation, one of the users offered to be partially in-volved in the "Happy Customers" circle to help us build the best possible version 5.0. Who would have thought that a customer would ever become part of one of our teams! Sarah was so impressed that she resolved to dis-cuss this with all our large and medium-sized clients and decided to join the "Happy Customers" circle too.

Kate and I stop talking about work until after dinner. As we enjoy our dessert, she suddenly says: "You know, Chris? I'm so glad that you decided to become the CEO."

"How come?" I ask.

"Well," Kate continues, "your energy level has clearly gone up, and I see a sort of renewed strength and alertness. I don't have a better word for it. It was all there in the past when we were younger, which is probably one of the qualities that made me fall in love with you in the first place. But in recent years you've had a lot less energy. I have only realized this now that I see it coming back."

I look at her.

"I'm glad you're noticing it too," I say. "I've also felt it recently."

"If you ask me, it's because you're back in touch with what you really want in life, with your mission."

I think about what Kate has said. She's very much into personal growth and consciousness, and she's convinced that our humanity is at a turning point — a transition toward a new kind of coexistence. I don't know how much to believe in this, but whatever we're doing at HRS feels really good. And it's a completely new way of looking at work, a way that I think is a lot better in the long run for our employees, clients and shareholders, and most likely for our planet too.

"Yes," I say finally, "you might be right. A lot of good things seem to be happening at HRS lately. I felt that today, for example, when we met with the "Better Collaboration" circle for the first time. The way we collaborated, with each of us contributing based on his or her own strengths, was awesome. We were a great example of the change we want to enable others to experience too."

S3 is a completely different way of looking at work and collaboration.

"We finished our domain description and very quickly came to an agreement about the strategy we want to use," I continue explaining. "We even had enough time left to put plenty of drivers in their appropriate backlogs and to respond to some of them. We've already created a role and a few work agreements, and defined a number of actions for our operations backlog. One of them is for Bernie to schedule S3 trainings at HRS. It's un-believable how much we accomplished in just a few hours."

I stop talking when I see Kate trying to suppress a laugh.

"That's exactly what I mean; your work is really giving you energy," she laughs, "you can't even stop talking about it."

I pout and we both burst out laughing.

26

TECHNICAL PROBLEMS

A few weeks later, Steve surprises me during one of our weekly conversations. Many of his people have become quite involved in the new circles around version 5.0 that we created during the driver mapping session. Version 4.0 has gone into production without any major glitches and is now almost ready to go into standard maintenance mode. This means that the work for his people on this version is almost done. Luckily, Steve didn't stop them from getting involved in the new circles around version 5.0, nor did he interfere much with their strategy and their daily organization. Steve's people mixing with those in my earlier teams who were already used to self-organizing worked really well. And on top of that, Bernie has been actively coaching these circles.

Based on the insights gained by the circle "Happy Customers" about the expectations of our customers, the "Architecture" circle has started improving the technical architecture, which requires drastic adjustments. The circle "Frequent Delivery" is working on automating the testing of installations so that working versions of our product can be delivered faster and more frequently. And a new circle has even been created, the "Building Circle", in which teams have already started with the actual programming of version 5.0. All this is music to my ears, but it makes Steve quite nervous, which I understand.

"Okay, Chris, I don't like to admit it," Steve explains, "but I'm beginning to see how the new circles will help us make a better version 5.0."

"Wow, Steve," I say. "I'm glad to hear that."

"Just a minute," he replies immediately. "This will also entail a number of serious problems that might kill the whole lot. On the one hand, I can't just let that happen. But on the other hand, I'm not allowed to interfere, because they are supposed to be self-organizing. I have no clue how to deal with this, Chris."

Steve looks at me. I see he is genuinely concerned.

"I'm trying to learn as much as possible and to give hints in individual conversations with my people, but so far, it has led to nothing," he says.

"Oh," I say. "Can you say more about this?"

Steve explains the problems he sees, and I'm surprised by how up to date he is on the technical level. According to him, there are some architectural choices that have been made that support automatic testing. However, they'll prove far too costly to maintain later on when we need to make frequent and specific adjustments for our larger clients. He explains all the details, and as far as I can follow, his concerns are justified. He names a few other potential problems, which also seem to require rather quick action.

When Steve is done, I sigh.

"I'd expected that those subjects would be picked up by the delegate circle," I say, giving Steve a questioning look.

"These problems don't show up on the agenda of the delegate circle, Chris," he says. "And not because of any ill will, because the circles do good work. They simply don't have an overview and therefore don't understand when they might be creating problems for each other."

"And so the problems pile up," he adds.

"Well, then it would be ideal if you joined the delegate circle, Steve," I say eagerly. "Your experience and technical insight are invaluable for the teams. And I think you would also like to dig into those difficult technical problems. Don't you think so?"

I see a glimmer in his eyes, but he is not so easily convinced.

"You could even be actively involved in the "Architecture" circle and help its representative in the delegate circle to bring the proper issues to the table," I offer.

"And the project planning and monitoring?" he asks.

"You can keep doing that. You don't have to be in the circle full time."

"I'll think about it," he says.

"That's good," I reply, hiding my eagerness. It's obvious that I shouldn't push it further for now. I'm already happy with the softening of his attitude. A few weeks ago, it would have been unthinkable for Steve to join a circle.

"Thanks for letting me know, Steve. I'll talk to the teams and bring the problems you mentioned to them as a driver."

"No, just a minute," Steve stops me.

I turn to him in surprise. Steve looks at the ground, takes a deep breath, looks at me and says, "I'll do it."

"You mean," I start asking.

"Yes, I'm the one who raised the issue and who knows the details. And I care about all this. So it's my responsibility to approach the teams."

I can't suppress a smile.

"That's really great, Steve," I say. "You certainly can explain this much better than I could."

I understand that this is a very important moment in his growth, and I want to be careful. Which is why I don't try to convince Steve to join the "Architecture" circle.

"Let me know if there is something I can help you with," I say.

"Good, I will," Steve answers. He seems relieved about this solution. And I'm delighted with this step too.

"Super, let's go for lunch," I suggest, ending our conversation.

Later that day, I receive an sms from Bernie. "Guess who just signed up for our next S3 course?"

I have no idea and send back a question mark.

A few seconds later the answer lands: "Steve. Great, eh?"

I'm perplexed. Steve? Wow, that's amazing. Steve can really contribute a lot to HRS, and it would be a shame if he left just because he can't find it in himself to work with the S3 principles. Relieved, I take a deep breath and call Bernie. I want to know more about this!

Bernie tells me that Steve had talked to him this afternoon. Apparently, he'd already approached the "Architecture" circle and calmly and constructively explained his concerns. He even offered to help them with the challenges.

"What?" I interrupt him. "Has Steve already joined the 'Architecture' circle?"

"No, not quite yet," Bernie chuckles. "Give him some time. He's really in the process of finding his way. It's all going to turn out all right."

"Amazing," I answer. "I wonder what caused him to change his mind."

"I'm afraid I might have something to do with it," Bernie admits, laughing. "Right from the beginning, I've had regular conversations with Steve. Somehow, I quickly gained his trust, and he often came up to me when I was walking around HRS. I mostly listened to him, with a coaching attitude, presenting him with a mirror that he gradually dared to look into. That was really courageous on his part, because it wasn't easy for him to embrace both the fact that you are the new CEO and the change that S3 entails at the same time. But that's exactly what he's doing now — because he sees the potential, both for the product and the company."

I'm speechless. I had no idea that Bernie and Steve had actually seen each other on several occasions.

"Are you still there, Chris?" Bernie asks.

"Yes, yes," I answer. "I'm just stunned and don't know what to say, except to thank you."

"As I just said," Bernie answers, "Steve did most of the work."

"Tell me," I ask, "are you by any chance secretly talking to Peter, too?"

"No, why?"

"Because he's become very quiet since the incident with the interview. I hardly see him any more. He still contributes to our meetings, but in a less outspoken way than before."

I hesitate.

"You know," I continue, "I've always had a strange feeling about Peter's role in our S3 story. And now I don't know what to think about it."

"And have you shared that feeling with him?" Bernie asks me.

"No, of course not," I say. "Why would I want to do that? It's only a gut feeling."

"Why wouldn't you?" Bernie asks. "What's the worst that could happen?"

I gulp.

"Hmm, I don't know. But Peter is somehow positioned above me because he sits on the board."

"So what?" Bernie asks. "That's one more reason to ask him."

I sigh. Of course, Bernie is right. But somehow, I'm really not looking forward to approaching Peter about it.

"Now I also understand what you just said about the mirror," I say. "Very nice," I add sarcastically.

Bernie laughs.

"It's up to you whether you want to look in it or not, Chris. See you soon."

27

CHRIS SECRETLY GETS TO WORK

"Sweetheart, what are you doing up so late? Aren't you coming to bed?" Kate's sleepy voice interrupts my thoughts and I look up from my computer.

"Are you not asleep yet?" I ask her. "It's already past midnight."

"No, I can't sleep," she answers as she comes up to me and puts her head on my shoulders.

"Are you programming?" she asks me incredulously.

I feel cornered.

"Well, yes, I guess so," I admit.

Kate laughs.

"It's been years since you last did this here at home. What are you doing?"

"Well, more and more circles are storing their domain descriptions, roles and agreements on our intranet. But it doesn't work so well, I find. And it's really important that all these things are visible to everyone and that they can easily be updated. That's why I wanted to build an application for it."

"And that's why you're staying up late to program?"

"Well, yes," I smile sheepishly.

Kate gives me a kiss.

"Keep going," she says. "I'm going back to bed."

"You're not upset, then?" I ask.

"No, not at all," she reassures me. "I told you that I think it is great that you're so energized by all that's happening at HRS. As long as you don't leave me go to bed alone every night, I think it's fantastic."

With a wink, Kate goes back upstairs. I lean over my keyboard again.

The following morning, I need an extra cup of coffee to wake up. I'd stayed up programming for half the night, just like in the old days. Only now it's much more tiring for me, I realize. However, my first attempts last night only got me more excited about the idea to support the implementation of S3 patterns with software. Next to making all agreements, roles and circles at HRS transparent, this could help to bring new drivers to the right domains. And perhaps we could even manage the various backlogs in this tool too.

"And does that mean you'll be programming this evening and tonight as well?" Kate asks, laughing, after I told her about my ideas about the S3 software.

"A part of me would really like to," I admit.

"It's okay with me," Kate answers. "But is this software then not actually also a driver? Or what do you call that again?"

"What do you mean?" I ask.

"It's obvious that this gives you plenty of energy and the desire to continue working on it. You are clearly convinced that this software can help HRS."

"Yes, right," I answer. "In that sense it could indeed be considered as a driver for HRS."

"And so S3 demands that you secretly work on this all by yourself?" Kate teases me, with a twinkle in her eye.

I begin to understand where she's going with this, but I keep countering: "S3 doesn't prescribe anything. The S3 patterns are designed to be modular so that you can just use what you need at any given moment. That's exactly the beauty of S3."

Kate plays along.

"Ah, I see," she says, with mock seriousness. "And you're now using the 'secretly-working-on-it-myself-pattern' to respond to this driver."

"Exactly," I answer.

Kate senses a hint of annoyance in my voice.

"It's okay, sweetheart," she reassures me. "I'm only teasing you."

"I know," I reply.

> The S3 patterns are designed to be modular so that you can just use what you need at any given moment.

"Good," she says cheerfully. "Could you clear the table for me? I have to leave."

She gives me a kiss and disappears into the bathroom to get ready.

I stay on to finish my coffee. Of course, Kate's right. I should actually bring this driver into the proper domain at HRS, where it ends up on the operations or governance backlog of the most relevant circle or role to take proper action.

In this case, I suppose that would be the "Better Collaboration" circle. I think that would be the appropriate domain in the organization to decide whether HRS wants to invest in a new piece of software for internal use. Maybe I'll have to bring my ideas to the table after all. Who knows, the others might find it interesting as well, and we can create a project around it. I'd love to continue working on it then. Last night, I realized how much I still enjoy building software.

But how crazy is that? A CEO who gets involved in programming? On the other hand, a key element of S3 is making sure that everyone has the opportunity to fully contribute and express their potential at work. And there's nothing wrong with combining different roles.

28

PETER

When I arrive at HRS a little later, I literally bump into Peter in the lobby.

This can't be a coincidence, I think. It was only yesterday that I'd expressed my concerns about him to Bernie.

After some small talk, I ask Peter to join me in a meeting room. I don't want to risk other people overhearing our conversation.

"I'd like to share a concern with you," I say, getting straight to the point. "Or better, a strange gut feeling that has been bothering me for a while. I've tried to ignore it, but yesterday Bernie helped me to understand that it's probably better to just let it out, if that's okay with you."

Peter leans back and looks at me suspiciously.

"Yes, why not?" he finally says.

I take a deep breath, trying to find the right words. I don't want to accuse Peter unjustly or come across as judgmental.

"Peter," I say, "I can't get a good sense of how you are and above all how you have felt during our recent meetings. Sometimes you are really enthusiastic, and sometimes not at all. And since all that commotion over the interview, I haven't seen much of you."

"But that's all water under the bridge now," Peter interrupts me. "You did a great job fixing the issue with the interview and the stock prices are back to normal." He moves back a bit further and looks at me in anticipation.

"Right," I continue, as calmly as I can, "and as I already said, I'm not blaming you for anything with regard to the interview. That's not what I'm talking about. But not knowing how you feel makes me anxious and insecure, Peter. And I need your support in this whole project. You are on the board, and you are the one responsible for the financial and legal aspects. This is really important."

I hesitate for a moment but then add: "And I know from Paul that you too had once hoped to take on the role of CEO, which also contributes to how I feel, to be honest."

"That's true," Peter admits. He seems to have relaxed a bit. "But Paul chose you for good reason, and I've accepted it, Chris. Paul knew exactly what he was doing."

I nod.

"And how is it for you now?" I ask.

Peter shrugs.

"Good," he says, without looking me in the eye. "I had to get somewhat used to it in the beginning, but I'm quite all right now."

Again, I have the feeling that he is not being entirely honest with me. Perhaps not even with himself, I suppose.

I try again. "Okay, one more question then: have you thought about Paul's question?"

"Which question?" Peter tenses up again. I realize that he knows full well what I mean.

"The one he asked when we saw each other after the interview was published," I answer.

"So it is about the interview. You just said that you weren't blaming me for it," Peter says, a bit more forcefully than necessary.

"And I really don't, Peter," I say, trying to reassure him. He is clearly getting agitated, but I decide to go through with it.

"Paul asked whether you needed some more explanation or help on the topic of self-organization or S3," I say as calmly as I can.

"I understand it quite well," he answers resolutely. "I was one of the first to follow the S3 courses that Bernie ran, remember?"

I nod again.

"Okay, let's stop this conversation right here then," I suggest. There's no point in pushing further.

Peter nods and gets up.

"I just hope that you are happy here at HRS, Peter," I sigh.

Peter looks at me, his eyes a bit softer now.

"Thank you, Chris. But I'll take care of that myself," he says. "Don't worry."
He leaves the room and I stay behind, feeling somewhat dejected. I don't know whether this was such a good idea. Maybe I should have kept quiet after all.

"It is what it is," I reassure myself out loud. "At least I was honest."

29

SARAH'S ENTHUSIASM

I don't have much time to dwell on Peter, because at that moment, Susan, Meg, Rob and Mateo rush into the room. All four work in Sarah's Sales and Marketing Department, which counts about 20 heads.

"May we talk to you in confidence?" Rob asks.

"Of course," I say.

They close the door and tell me excitedly and all at once what has been happening in their department over the past weeks. Apparently, Sarah has instructed them to fully implement S3 in the whole department. They now have seven circles and 18 roles, and Sarah's people are thoroughly confused. They're lost in all the backlogs and meetings, and everyone has had enough of it.

"That doesn't sound good," I say when they've finished. "And you're the lucky ones who get to tell me about it?"

"Well," Susan says. "We tried to tell Sarah, but she doesn't seem to understand what we mean."

"Typical of Sarah," I chuckle. Sarah has told me recently about their progress in implementing S3, but in her version everything went just fine.

"Sarah is probably so enthusiastic about S3 that she wants to move too far, too quickly and forgets to take you along in this whole process, right?" I ask them.

"Probably, yes," Mateo sighs. He is one of the older account managers. "We know she has the best intentions, but meanwhile, we have to deal with it. All this S3 stuff takes so much time that we don't get a chance to do our actual work."

"Hmm," I say. "And effectiveness is precisely one of the principles in S3."

All four look at me expectantly. But I'm not ready to pull their bacon out of the fire. That would just cement the old way of managing and controlling, and that's the last thing I want.

"I'm not going to solve the problem for you," I say. "You'll have to do it yourselves. But I do want to help. Tell me what I can do."

They look at one another. Susan finally says: "Perhaps you could help us explain this to Sarah."

"Perhaps," I hesitate. Even though I know Sarah quite well, and I'm sure that she doesn't consider me as her superior in such a conversation, I still want to be cautious. I want people to learn to take care of themselves. By becoming involved in that conversation, I may be giving the wrong signal.

"What would you like to achieve when you talk to Sarah?" I ask them. "What would a good conversation with Sarah look like?"

Mateo looks at his colleagues and then says: "That she listens to our side of the story, without overreacting."

"And that she won't dismiss our concerns in all her enthusiasm," Rob adds. "I suppose that she simply doesn't realize how confusing all this is for us."

"Okay," I say. "Makes sense. And why has that not worked so far?"

Susan chuckles. "I think that the last time we were in her office, we were there like a bunch of headless chickens, unable to bring our story across."

"I think that's it," Rob sighs. "We also don't know S3 well enough to put our finger on the problem. Everything Sarah tells us about circles and roles sounds logical — until you find yourself sitting in three circles and four roles."

Right at that moment, I see Bernie coming down the corridor. Our guardian angel. There's no such thing as coincidence.

"Do you think a neutral facilitator who's thoroughly familiar with S3 could be helpful?" I ask. "Because Bernie's here today. Maybe he has time to help you?"

The four of them nod happily, so I call Bernie to join us.

They explain the situation to him, a bit more calmly and constructively now. Bernie listens patiently. I notice how, through his questions and reactions, he helps them to gain insight not only into their own needs but also those of

Sarah. They finally decide to talk to Sarah again, this time with Bernie as a neutral facilitator.

"Great," I say. "Good luck."

I'm no longer worried about this conversation. With Bernie by their side, everything will be fine, I'm sure.

And it seems I'm right. When I call Bernie on my way home, he tells me that together with Sarah, they managed to quickly dissect the problem and have already taken some first steps to resolve it.

He explains how Sarah had created several circles and roles without first listing and prioritizing any drivers. And since her team doesn't have much of a grasp of S3 yet, they were unable to push back. Good intentions, combined with overenthusiasm and wanting to do too much too fast, was Bernie's conclusion. And pushing things down onto her team instead of inviting people to co-create and run experiments in response to actual organizational needs that they are facing. Two typical pitfalls in implementing S3 patterns.

Circles and roles should be a conscious response to a driver and domain. But it's unnecessary to define a domain and create a separate, formal role or circle for every driver, especially in a small team such as the Sales and Marketing Department.

As a result of the conversation, Sarah and her team will roll back on everything and start over with a brief workshop to list and prioritize their current drivers. In the next Sales and Marketing meeting, they'll start with the most important drivers first and go from there.

Bernie explains to me that there's typically a lot of wisdom behind how a team is already set up. Therefore, it's valuable to start where you are, and focus on the priority issues, rather than to just make changes for the sake of it. This way, you're more likely to build on what's already working, rather than unwittingly disable yourself and create a series of new problems instead. He suspects that Sarah's team will end up with far fewer changes this time around, and certainly fewer circles and roles. And by involving the employees in the decision making from the start, they'll take more ownership of whatever is decided too.

Bernie's been very present at HRS over the past few weeks. At some point in the past, I talked to him about compensating him properly for his work, but he refused. As his help is invaluable to us, I bring up the subject again.

"I really enjoy my work here," he assures me. "And I'm learning a lot myself. By talking to people who make mobile software and observing how they work, I'm getting a deeper understanding of agile and lean than I had before. This is an area where your teams are more advanced than we are at The Facts."

"Okay," I say. "Well that's good to know. Still, I'd like to give something back for all you do. But I don't have the slightest idea what."

"You know what I'd really appreciate?" Bernie says after a few seconds of reflection. "Once HRS is fully back on its feet, you could share your insights and experiences with the world. That way, more teams and organizations can benefit from S3 and the insights you've gained around implementing S3 patterns."

"I promise, Bernie," I say earnestly, although I'm not yet quite sure how.

"Oh, and something else," Bernie adds. "I'd appreciate a peer review about my role in your organization."

"A what?"

"A peer review. It's a really useful S3 pattern that we haven't pulled in yet. We brought up the topic when we selected Peter as the spokesperson. I've been wanting to explain more about it but because it hasn't come up since, I didn't get around to it."

"Ah, yes, I remember," I say. "How does that work again?"

> **DEFINITION**
>
> *Peer reviews help to continuously improve the way individuals and groups account for their domain.*

"Well," Bernie explains, "it's a meeting designed to evaluate both a domain and how a role keeper or a team are working to account for it. It's an opportunity to celebrate what's going well and to learn how to improve in future. The result is an actionable Development Plan that guides future improvements that the individual or team can make."

"Ah," Bernie adds, "and by the way, it's the responsibility of the person or group being reviewed to initiate their peer review and to decide who they want to invite as participants. Unless there are any specific individuals named by the delegator in the domain description, of course."

I think for a moment.

"Considering the principle of accountability and equivalence, that sounds logical to me," I say.

"Right," Bernie confirms.

"I guess you don't want to explain the details of this pattern to me now?" I ask, knowing the answer full well.

"No, let's learn by doing," Bernie confirms my assumption. "I'll organize my peer review in the coming days. And I'll invite you too, of course."

"You said you select the participants yourself. Who else will you invite?" I ask.

"Usually, you'd invite people you frequently work with or those who are impacted by your work, such as people from the superset circle or those who answer to you. You might even invite clients. If you think it's valuable, you could even invite your mother," Bernie laughs.

We end our conversation and I look forward to the invitation to Bernie's peer review. I suspect that Julia will find this a very interesting pattern too.

30

BERNIE'S PEER REVIEW

The following Monday, Bernie's peer review is scheduled for immediately after our meeting with the management team. Present in the circle are Bernie, myself, Julia, Sarah, Steve, Bjorn from Carlos's team as well as Elena and Tina from HR.

"There were so many people I could have asked," Bernie explains. "To avoid too big a party, I decided to invite those of you I've worked with who have shown most interest in S3. That way, you'll get to know this pattern and can experiment with it yourself, if you'd like."

I smile. Typical Bernie.

"If you are the one choosing the participants in your peer review, aren't you pretty much steering the outcome?" Tina asks.

It's useful to get honest feedback as early as possible.

"Well," Bernie answers, "it does require some integrity to bring together an objective group. But imagine you don't do that, because you're trying to avoid less favorable feedback for some reason. This will inevitably lead to tension afterwards. These tensions will then lead to drivers on your role or team's backlog, if people are navigating via tension. It's much better to get honest feedback as early as possible, so you learn from it and use it to continuously develop and improve."

We nod. Bernie explains the objective of a peer review once more and suggests that we go about it step by step.

"The first step after bringing the group together should be to refresh the domain description and the strategy of the role. Because that's what the conversation will subsequently be all about. Typically you would send out the domain description in advance so that people have some time to reflect before the meeting."

"In my case, however," Bernie continues, "there was no formal description of my role to consider, because we never established one. So, I just made a summary of how I interpreted my role here, mainly for the purpose of this peer review."

Bernie shows us a sheet that he's prepared. On it, he's written: *"HRS is facing difficulties and wants to become more agile and effective as an organization. To do so, they would like help in understanding and applying S3 principles and patterns throughout the organization."*

Below the driver is a short list of key responsibilities, such as sharing his experience and explaining the theory as well as helping to put it into practice. As for the constraints of the domain, Bernie states that he works with us voluntarily and without obligation; that he only works with people or teams when invited; and that he'll never oblige anyone to do anything.

Together, we go over the role domain description. No one has an objection to it.

"Great," Bernie says, handing out some Post-its and markers. "Then we can continue with the next step. I asked you to prepare by reflecting on what you appreciate about my work here at HRS and what you would suggest I could further improve on. Let's start with collecting the appreciations, meaning positive feedback. I propose we spend one or two minutes to check your preparation and individually reflect on what you appreciate in how I'm working to fulfill this role. Please write down each appreciation on a separate Post-it note. Clearly legible and summarized in a few words."

"Can I ask something first?" Sarah stops him. "We should write down appreciations, while I thought we were about to create a development plan. Isn't that about points for improvement?"

"That's right," Bernie smiles. "And we'll get to those in a minute. But recognizing what you are doing well and what you should continue doing, or do more of, is also an important part of a peer review."

"That makes sense," Julia confirms. "You also acknowledge all the hard work and the qualities of the person in question. That's really important as a basis for being able and willing to further improve as well."

"Quite right," Bernie nods. "And why do you think I should be the one to share appreciations first?"

Again, Julia responds: "Because it invites self-reflection?"

"Exactly," Bernie says. "This is an important skill. And it also invites you to take responsibility for your own behavior and development. It's not only feedback from others, but above all your own feedback that will form the basis of your development plan."

A peer review invites taking responsibility for one's own behavior and development.

"Yes," Bjorn agrees, "and often you know for the most part what's going well and what isn't. The others can then confirm or add to it from there."

"Right," Bernie says. "So, let's start."

We start writing down appreciations on Post-it notes until Bernie proposes that we start sharing them. Bernie begins by telling us that he truly enjoyed being able to contribute at HRS, and that he's actively invested in his own learning throughout the process. He values the fact that the first concrete and positive results are starting to show in the organization and that he's operated within the constraints of his domain throughout. While talking, Bernie sticks his Post-it notes on the flip chart, so we can all clearly see them.

Next, Bernie invites us to use rounds to share appreciations one by one, immediately sticking them to the flip chart and using "bingo" to avoid unnecessary duplicates. Sarah goes first, as she is sitting next to Bernie. She thinks that Bernie was very present and highly flexible, which meant that he was available when it was most important.

We go around the circle and everyone adds what he or she appreciated, nearly filling the entire sheet.

"That's really great to hear," Bernie says, with a twinkle in his eye. "Many thanks. Let's stop the meeting right here."

I cringe for a moment, but quickly understand that he's kidding. We all laugh. The next step in a peer review is to collect improvement suggestions. Again, we first individually reflect and summarize our ideas for improvement on Post-its. After preparing a new flip chart sheet, Bernie shares all the suggestions for improvement that he sees for himself.

He says that his colleagues at The Facts didn't have a good overview of when he would be available at their office and neither did people at HRS, at times. He suggests finding a way to synchronize and share his calendars. He also thinks it would have been useful to have worked with us to clarify his domain more explicitly before now, probably even at the start of his engagement. Therefore, he intends to put more S3 patterns in practice in relation to his own involvement at HRS.

"Let's go the other way around the circle," Bernie suggests when he's done, looking at Sarah. She has no suggestions for improvement and passes. Tina, the next one in the circle, shares that she would value more documentation on S3.

"You have a great way of explaining the S3 patterns," she says. "And your facilitation is fantastic. But you won't be around forever, and I'd like to refer back to the things we learned from you whenever I want to try out something myself. Like the practical tips that you give when you facilitate a pattern."

"I understand," Bernie nods. "And what's the improvement you'd like to suggest?"

"That, together with us, you'll find a way to document what we learn from you and to make it accessible to us," Tina replies.

We continue to go around the circle, sticking our improvement suggestions on the flip chart.

Peer review

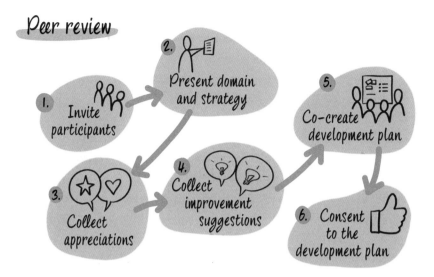

When we're done, Bernie explains the next step to us.

"Based on all of this, we can now co-create a development plan," he says. "To do so, I take the lead, as it's my review, and you support me. We can either do it together, here and now, or I take all this information with me, come up with a proposal myself and then bring it back to this group to check for any objections or concerns. Once we've agreed on the development plan between us, I would then present it to my delegator too, to check with them if they have any further objections or concerns."

"I'm not sure I understand that last part," Elena says.

"Well, first there has to be consent from the group that carries out the peer review," Bernie explains. "In this case, that's you. But because people choose who they invite to their peer review, it's possible that not all delegators are present. So, by presenting the development plan as a proposal to the delegator too, it gives them the opportunity to input by way of any objections or concerns they may have."

Elena nods.

You need to check for consent on the development plan with the delegator, as he holds the final responsibility for the primary driver of the domain.

"I check with my delegator for consent to my development plan, just as I would with my strategy too, because that's where the final responsibility for the primary driver of my domain lies. Is that clearer now?" Bernie asks as he looks around.

Everyone nods.

"It makes sense," Julia replies. "But you have to really pay attention."

We laugh. I'm thinking that the S3 software that I'm secretly creating could help to support this kind of thing as well.

We decide to work on the development plan together, focusing on the most important points for improvement. Bernie explains that a good development plan consists of three parts. The first part deals with the personal development plan of the individual or group being reviewed. Along with that, the development plan could include recommended changes to the domain that was evaluated and finally, potential adjustments to the way the primary driver of the domain is described.

> **DEFINITION**
>
> A development plan contains both a personal development plan as well as improvements to the domain and its primary driver.

Bernie reminds us that this development plan will remain a proposal until consent has been reached with the delegator.

Ten minutes later, the development plan is finished. One of the actions is to set up the automatic synchronization of Bernie's calendars. Bjorn will help Bernie with it, with the evaluation criteria being how his colleagues at The Facts rate the predictability of his presence in the future.

We added that Bernie will lend his support in documenting our insights around S3 to the role domain description. Concrete ideas and actions around that include summarizing relevant information and recording it on video, as well as making important S3 patterns and the way they're facilitated available.

We finally take the last step in a typical peer review, which is checking for consent to the development plan. Since everyone had worked on it, all thumbs go up. Bernie says that he'll do the same in the management team, which he considers as the delegator for his role.

"I'm glad I came," Julia says in the closing round. "I think I'll introduce this in my team; I can see how it adds a lot of value. Who knows, it might just complement our assessment and performance reviews."

"Or replace them," I say, only half jokingly.

"That won't be easy," Julia thinks out loud. But she looks excited, and can barely suppress a smile.

"Just wait and see what your first experiments will bring," Bernie laughs. "Step by step. And always pull in patterns in response to concrete drivers that emerge and are qualified and prioritized. Navigate via tension, remember?"

"I still have a question," Tina says. "You said a team can do a peer review too. How does that work exactly?"

Bernie responds: "In that case, the feedback is about your collaboration as a team in responding to the domain's primary driver."

"And who should be included there?" Julia asks.

"Well, the whole team, plus whoever else they decide to invite," Bernie explains. "This might include delegators, people who answer to them, people from neighboring domains, or customers. Anything is possible."

"Any other questions?" Bernie asks when he sees that we have grasped his explanation.

"Yes, does anyone want some coffee?" Elena giggles.

We laugh. Bernie thanks us all again for the feedback, and with that we conclude our very first peer review at HRS.

31

COOKING WITH KATE

"How was your day?" Kate asks me in the evening while we're in the kitchen cooking together.

"Really good," I say. "Our management meetings are becoming more fun by the week — and more meaningful too."

"Super," Kate responds. "Tell me about it."

I tell her about our governance meeting today, Bernie's peer review and how the afternoon was fun and worthwhile too because of an interesting conversation with Paul. Version 4.0 is now in production, and it seems that our clients are quite satisfied with it. And the typical teething problems inherent in a new version have finally been solved as well.

There haven't been enough clients switching to version 4.0 to call it a success, and the delay of the release has cost us considerable trust on the stock market. Slowly and surely, the damage is being controlled. So today, we followed up on what's still needed before Paul can leave his role as CEO once and for all. I have learned a lot from him in the past weeks, and I'm glad that he took all the time necessary to transfer everything to me in the way he did.

We decided that Paul will stay another week at HRS to complete the transfer. He'll assign as many of the remaining issues as possible to the right people on the work floor or to the management team, to the extent that they belong there. During the transition phase, Paul and I very consciously studied where all the different parts of his job as CEO needed to go within the organization. We looked at them as drivers that have to be passed to the right domains. Of course, some of his responsibilities will stay with me, but only those that I'm competent in and that I really want to take on. It was great to see how the traditional definition of a CEO changes in practice when approaching it with S3 principles and a more sociocratic mindset.

"That sounds really good, Chris," Kate says when I finally finish talking. "I hadn't expected Bernie's ideas to impact HRS so quickly and profoundly."

"Not so fast," I say, trying to put things in perspective. "The actual work is yet to be done. Up until now, we've only really experimented within the old management team and a few new circles next to that. It's true, this is bearing fruit quite quickly. But the rest of the organization hasn't changed yet. Our old organizational structure and functions are still in place, and I suspect that this will soon create tension around the new roles, compensation, and so on. And until version 5.0 is successfully delivered, I daren't speak of success."

"Yes, okay," Kate says. "I understand. But I wouldn't underestimate the extent to which your experiments are already having an influence on the whole organization. This is systemic. You can't do something in one part of a system without affecting the whole. It's like putting a few drops of milk into a cup of coffee; it changes the color of the coffee forever."

Every experiment or change influences the whole system.

I chuckle. "Watch out, sweetheart. You're starting to sound like Bernie."

Kate sticks her tongue out at me. "I'll take that as a compliment," she says.

32

MEANWHILE

"Chris, how nice to see you," Paul says as he walks into the restaurant. We shake hands. It's been nearly two months since Paul finished transferring his role as CEO to me. Except for a few short, business-oriented phone calls, we've not spoken since. It was high time for us to sit down together to catch up.

After the waiter has taken our orders, Paul jumps in to ask how things have developed at HRS. I tell him that I'm pretty happy with how everything is going. Of course, we have issues from time to time with our new way of working, and occasionally we fall back into some of our old habits. But overall, it's going well, I tell Paul. And it looks like some important pieces of the puzzle are falling into place.

One of these puzzle pieces is Steve. He gradually adopted our new way of working and is growing into it. He decided to become part of the "Architecture" circle, where he serves as a critical eye and, based on his many years of experience, is now actively working on the technical architecture. His attitude has become considerably more positive and constructive lately, which also earns him a lot more recognition from other employees.

This is partly the reason why we were able to take some major steps in the technical field. Solid automation of testing and installing our product allows us to deliver stable versions more frequently. Over time, this means a significant reduction in lead time to our customers.

The work of the "Architecture" and "Frequent Delivery" circles began to overlap so much that they decided to merge. They retained the name "Frequent Delivery", because the required architectural changes all went in that direction.

Here too, Steve was the driving force, and positively so. And it's a great example of how easily an organization's structure can be adapted based on real needs.

A lot has also happened in the "Building" circle, which now consists of four fully-fledged teams. The teams decided to use a number of S3 patterns, especially those coming from the agile world. They first built a backlog for the product, which is a prioritized list of small pieces of the product, each of which, upon completion, are adding value to HRS or to our clients. Next, they introduced short iterations to develop and deliver these product increments. Each iteration starts with a Planning Meeting. This means that, for an upcoming period of two weeks, they plan together what they're able to accomplish, thereby maximizing value for our customers. The teams get together briefly each day to check whether enough progress is being made. They call it a Daily Standup. At the end of each iteration, the teams conduct a Review Meeting along with their colleagues from the "Happy Customers" circle. It's during these meetings that they evaluate the new pieces of work they've completed and how their new insights can serve to improve the product in the following iterations.

Additionally, the teams organize a Retrospective at the end of each iteration too. There, they reflect on their collaboration, examining what went well and what did not, to identify concrete points for improvement.

All these S3 patterns originate from the agile philosophy and development frameworks such as Scrum. My old department has been familiar with those for years, which has been of great help to the "Building" circle. As a result, the work of the "Building" circle is now so far ahead that we'll be able to deliver version 5.0 much sooner than expected. Instead of taking nearly a year to come up with a new version, as we did with version 4.0, delivery time is now five months. Naturally, version 5.0 will have fewer new functionalities, but we're certain that the technical quality will be better, which means fewer complaints and repairs. From now on, the intention is to release a new version at least every three months.

More importantly, we're now confident that nearly all of our clients will find version 5.0 valuable enough to purchase. That's largely due to the great work of the "Happy Customers" circle. Sarah and her team were able to convince a few other big clients to free up time to help them in identifying their real needs and learning how we could best meet them. Having learned from previous mistakes, we now keep all our customers continuously updated. Consequently, all our clients know what to expect in version 5.0 and we are making sure it addresses their most important requirements.

Just recently, Sarah told me with a big smile how some of our most difficult clients have become fans of our products — even though version 5.0 won't be released for another eight weeks.

A significant contribution to all of that was the work of the "Better Collaboration" circle. Together with Bernie, the team made sure that everyone working with S3 at HRS had the opportunity to learn to implement the principles and techniques correctly. Bernie facilitated several S3 workshops and training sessions and worked especially closely with a few of the more enthusiastic fans of S3 to become internal S3 coaches. He gave them on-the-job training, and together they're doing a thorough job of spreading S3-related knowledge and experience within HRS.

But if that weren't enough, nearly everyone in the organization has quite organically begun to experiment with S3 patterns in one way or another. Especially patterns such as navigate via tension, consent decision making, co-creating proposals, peer review, and the various patterns related to iterative planning and delivery of work. Individuals and teams are collaborating together so much better..

I tell Paul all this, and it makes him laugh.

"So, all the agile practices that you've been using all along are now spreading throughout HRS?"

"Well, yes, actually," I say. "They've even begun using some of these patterns in the financial department. And of course, my old team members from the mobile software department have a lot of experience in these kind of things, even more than Bernie himself, so they've become a real asset in the transformation."

"Hear, hear," Paul chuckles. "I knew it was the right thing to ask you to become the CEO."

I blush.

"Let's not jump to conclusions until version 5.0 is out the door," I say. "But so far, it's looking good. I have the impression that the atmosphere at HRS is a lot more pleasant than a few months ago. And many colleagues are saying the same thing too."

I tell Paul that several other things seem to me to be falling into place too. We recently reformulated the role of CEO to fit more coherently with the S3 principles while still meeting all legal and regulatory needs. I'm getting into the "groove" of the role now and hardly ever need to deal with things that don't interest me or that others can take care of more effectively than I can. I'd never dreamed it could be possible when I accepted Paul's offer those few months ago.

What I'm most thrilled about is my idea to support S3 with specific software. It took me another couple of evenings' work on it at home before I was convinced of its potential. I then brought it as a driver to the "Better Collaboration" circle, where we decided to invest in an initial version for internal use. The software is designed to support HRS employees in bringing their drivers to the proper roles or teams. The new application will help to manage drivers, domains, teams, roles and backlogs in a transparent manner.

And so, two weeks ago, I joined three other colleagues in a new circle that is working on the S3 software. I now spend about one third of my time working on the software, and I love being able to program again and to conceive and build a new application with others. I could not have imagined this would be possible either, at the beginning of our experiment with S3 at HRS.

Paul smiles broadly as he listens to my report.

"I'm really happy for you and HRS," he says. I can tell by his expression that he genuinely means it. "Thank you for taking over the helm, Chris. You're doing a fantastic job."

"All right, all right," I say, "others could have accomplished the same thing, you know. I haven't done that much. Most of the changes have come from the people themselves. And Bernie helped us tremendously."

"Yes, maybe," Paul responds. "But you created the context in which it all became possible — just by being the way you are and living by what you stand for. You're a believer in self-organization and the principles of S3. Not only on a rational level, but because it comes naturally to you to give your people freedom and to trust in their potential and in the patterns of S3. For myself and many others, it would be a struggle to let go as you did and to trust that others could pick up the reins."

I nod. "Thanks, Paul," I say. I'm pleased to receive Paul's recognition.

"As I said, Chris: thank you," Paul answers, laughing. "If version 5.0 becomes as successful as it looks right now, it will lift HRS out of a really difficult situation."

"And we've all contributed to that," I say proudly.

33

PETER'S RESIGNATION

As I walk back to HRS after my lunch with Paul, I get an sms from Peter, asking whether he could still see me today. I tell him that I'll be at the office in 15 minutes and that I have time for him. I'm curious as to what could suddenly be so urgent. I hope nothing went wrong again with an interview or some other formal communication.

After getting some coffee and finding a meeting room, Peter gets straight to the point.

"Chris, it took me a long time to come to this decision, but I'm going to leave HRS and look for another challenge elsewhere."

"What?" I'm perplexed. I hadn't seen that coming.

"Sorry, Chris," Peter says. "I really tried, but I can't do it."

"Wait a minute," I stammer. "I don't understand. What is it you can't do? And what do you mean, leave HRS?"

Peter smiles at my confusion, but his eyes look sad.

"I'm giving notice," Peter explains. He pauses for a while, waiting for my reaction.

I nod. At this moment, I don't know what else to say or do.

"You know that I've had issues with your new approach since the beginning," Peter goes on. "I understood that Paul was right in choosing you, that HRS needed a breath of fresh air, but I never truly believed in your ideas, Chris. And lately, I realized that deep down I had expected that we would go back to our old ways within a few weeks. I didn't expect you or S3 to change this company and its culture so much."

He looks me in the eye. I've never seen Peter so authentic. I nod to encourage him to go on.

"But that's what happened. First in our management team and then with all the teams and departments too. The incident with the interview showed me in retrospect that HRS was already in the process of change but that I wasn't yet convinced about your new ideas."

Peter pauses again.

"I fooled myself into thinking that because I'm responsible for the finances, I could hold on to my former role and way of working and that your ideas would only apply to the development teams. But that didn't last long. My people also started to experiment with S3 techniques and to ask me questions. For example, they wanted a lot more transparency on the figures and loans and also wanted to make more decisions jointly instead of leaving them up to me. And so, unwittingly, they questioned my role. Or rather, my position."

"Your position?" I ask.

"Yes," Peter answers. "In the past I've made a lot of financial decisions on my own. As the financial manager, I'm the only one who has a complete overview on all sorts of figures and I like it that way because then many decisions and responsibilities end up with me. It made me indispensable at HRS and gave me energy and fulfillment. I know it's a bit old school, but that's how I've worked all my life and it complements who I am. For several months now, I've desperately tried to change, mostly myself, but without success. And to be really honest, I realize that I don't want to."

"Gosh, Peter," I say. "I didn't know that this was so fundamental to you."
Peter nods.

"I know," he sighs. "I covered it up, even from myself in some ways, because I didn't want to admit it. For example, in our conversation when you asked me whether anything was the matter. I no longer want that."

"I'm glad, Peter," I say. "I'm really thankful that you're being so honest with me — and with yourself."

We remain silent for a while. Neither of us knows what to say.

"And now?" I finally break the silence.

"I don't want to leave here, slamming doors," Peter answers. "On the contrary. I want to sit down with you and my team to figure out how I can leave as quickly as possible without creating any big issues. Because even though I don't fit in here, I'm beginning to believe that your new approach is actually working. It seems to have been the right decision for HRS."

"That's great, Peter," I say. "It won't be easy to make up for your financial expertise and the many years of experience you have. And so I'm happy that you want to help us with that."

"Yes, for sure," Peter continues. "And I'd like to keep my position on the board, which will keep me involved in HRS. That way, I can also share my knowledge with you if and when you ask for it, without having to interfere and control everything on the work floor."

"And what do you want to do in the future?" I ask. "Have you already thought about that?"

"No," Peter says. "I haven't thought about it yet. First, I want to bring everything to an end here. But I do want to stay active. I'm too young to retire. I guess I'll need to find a more traditional company that's looking for a financial director who's more old school."

We both laugh at Peter's last comment. It lightens up the conversation. We keep talking a bit more about how we'll manage the handover and the best way to communicate his decision.

Even though I'm somewhat shaken by his unexpected news, I can already feel how, in the end, it will be good for HRS and for Peter. His personality and qualities will probably be better matched to a different environment, and he'll be happier there as well.

On my way home, I immediately call Bernie. I tell him about Peter's decision and he doesn't seem too surprised.

"I'm not going to pretend that I saw this coming," Bernie explains, "but it's no real surprise either. Peter is very concerned about individual performance and image. And controlling all the details. And the latter certainly clashes with the S3 principles and self-organization."

"Yes," I respond. "He admitted himself that he had trouble letting go of control and having the transparency we expect. He said he tried to change, but that he couldn't manage."

"It's not easy, Chris," Bernie says. "Such strong personal values and patterns are hard to change. And some of us find it easier than others."

I'm thinking of Steve. He's managed to find his own way in our new approach. And what's more, he now contributes based on his own strengths and less out of fear and the need for control.

"It's too bad for HRS, I think," Bernie continues. "Because along with his shortcomings, HRS also loses Peter's good qualities. There's nothing wrong with Peter's focus on results and figures. On the contrary."

I completely agree with Bernie. It is great that Peter was able to make his decision so calmly and consciously, and that, in the end, he wants to ensure a proper and undramatic handover, just like Paul did.

34

CHAMPAGNE

"Let's toast the successful launch of version 5.0," says Bob, the chairman of the board, raising his glass.

"And to the rescue of HRS," Paul adds. He winks at me as we clink our glasses.

We don't usually start our board meetings with champagne, but this time it's fitting. Version 5.0 came on the market successfully two weeks ago, and our clients are more than happy with it. Our stock prices also reflect this handsomely. We've even attracted a few new clients for our product, including a really big player on the market. HRS has made the necessary transformation and is a successful company again.

"Chris," Bob says, "could you briefly tell us how version 5.0 came about? And what happened since you've been at the helm of HRS. I think it's important that we understand what's been going on in a bit more detail."

"Of course," I say. "But first I'd like to point out that I'm not the only one responsible for this change. We did this together with all our HRS colleagues. So I would like to put a celebration with the whole company on the agenda."

Bob nods and makes a note to himself about my new agenda item.

I tell the other board members what has transpired since Paul's resignation. I try to give them the feeling of how the structure and collaboration at HRS has become increasingly flexible, continuously adapting to our organizational needs as they have emerged. I also tell them how the employees have assumed more accountability for their work and the HRS product line, as they were able to work more in line with their passion and their intrinsic motivation in their new roles, circles and other types of teams that emerged. I explain the principles and some important S3 patterns so that the board is more in touch with them. Their questions tell me that they're sincerely

SOCIOCRACY 3.0 – THE NOVEL

interested. The successful release of version 5.0 seems to have convinced them of our rather unusual approach.

Before I come to the end of my speech, I tell them about the new initiatives that have seen the light lately. For example, in consultation with our clients, we'll bring a new version of our product onto the market every quarter. From a technical point of view, we're ready for that.

In addition, a new circle was created to experiment with a new type of service supporting our product. The driver for it came out of the "Happy Customers" circle, when they realized that some of our clients were interested not only in our product, but also in our new way of working. And so the idea of bringing a bit of HR consultancy onto the market on the topic of "Thriving Workplaces" was born, based on S3 and our own experiences.

I'm personally really happy with this initiative. I think it will mean a lot to HRS in the future. Besides the commercial value, it's my hope that we can continue to redefine our mission and that, in time, we'll not only offer the best HR solution, but that we can support other organizations to become better places to work in too. Organizations in which people are more fulfilled and collaborate consciously and intentionally to do great things for the world.

Bob, who chairs the meeting, thanks me for all that information and asks whether there are any more questions.

"Yes," Paul says. "We all seem to be convinced about the new way of working at HRS, right?"

He looks around the room and everyone nods.

"So how can we as the board support this actively in the long run?" Paul asks. "I think it is important, because today we have Chris, who is putting his stamp on the organization, but you don't know what might happen in the years to come. In the end, we're the ones responsible for the future of HRS. And this seems to be the right approach for our company."

"True," Bob nods.

"Should we not try to use the S3 patterns in our meetings too?" asks Emily, an older woman I don't know very well yet.

All eyes are on me. I swallow. I know that the active support of the board for our new way of working is crucial in the long run, but I had not expected to talk about it today. I was already happy with the first signs of interest the board members had shown in S3.

"Ahem, yes," I say. "That would be fantastic. And, in fact, very important, as Paul said."

We agree to offer a short S3 training to all board members, combined with a visit to several teams in HRS. This will show the board members what S3 looks like in practice. Bob also asks me to facilitate the next board meeting and to see which S3 patterns we could apply. A challenge I'm glad to take on.

After the meeting, I walk out with Paul.

"Do you still have a minute?" he asks. "Because I'd like to ask you something outside the professional context."

"Of course."

"Well," Paul hesitates. "My wife and I, together with the family of my oldest daughter and some other people, have this dream of a co-housing project. We want to live together with a number of families and to share a few things with one another, like the garden, the garage and common spaces. This is very appealing to us, both from a social and an ecological point of view."

"Interesting," I say.

"Indeed, but not so easy. We're in the process of making plans together with six families. We meet on a regular basis and are working out the details in working groups. But it's cumbersome. We're talking about fundamental decisions, such as how we want to live together, what land we want to buy and how to settle it all financially."

"Okay," I say. I still don't understand exactly where Paul is going with this.

He sees my puzzled look and comes to the point: "I'd like to ask you to come and teach us about S3. Our work groups are actually some type of circle, I assume, which need to confer with one another. And learning to make decisions by consent will save us a lot of energy. Would you like to guide us in this, as some kind of coach? A bit like Bernie did at HRS?"

"Ahem," I stammer. His question had taken me by surprise.

"Why don't you think about it?" Paul suggests.

"No need," I say. "I didn't expected that question, so I was a bit stunned. But I'm happy to do it, Paul. It's a great honor. And I'll learn a lot from this experience myself, I'm sure."

"Super," Paul says.

As I get into my car later on, I realize that I'm fulfilling a promise that I made to Bernie, the promise to further spread S3. I laugh and send Bernie an sms. When he answers me with a smiley, I message him back: "Would you like to join Kate and me for dinner next Sunday? I want to toast S3 and to thank you for the journey that we've taken together. 6pm?"

He responds immediately: "Gladly. I'll bring champagne. See you on Sunday!"

35

S3 SOFTWARE

Dinner with Bernie on Sunday night passes in a flash. The three of us have a great time and talk about all kinds of topics. Of course, we also bring up S3 and HRS. Bernie and I are extremely glad that S3 found such strong resonance at HRS, and we're both proud of the results of the various teams.

We also chat about the S3 software that we're in the process of building. We launched a first basic version, which most of the circles at HRS are now using. It seems much more practical than trying to keep everything on the intranet and in our calendars.

After dessert and coffee, Bernie gets ready to go home.

"I have a surprise for you," I hold him back.

Bernie sits down again, and I present him with a big green envelope.

"Here, for you. As a thank-you for all that you've taught us, both in tangible and intangible ways."

Bernie looks at me in surprise.

"You really didn't have to, Chris," he says, but his smile tells me that he's happy with my gesture. He rips open the envelope and pulls out a card. On it is the logo that we created for the S3 software and a URL.

Bernie looks puzzled.

"The S3 software?" Bernie asks? "And a link?"

"Yep," I say. "I've put the last version of the S3 software online, and you can download it for free on this URL."

"What do you mean?" Bernie asks. He gives me another confused look. "So we can use it at The Facts? That would indeed be fantastic."

"For example," I say, with a mysterious smile.

"C'mon on, Chris," Kate butts in, laughing. "Just tell him."

"Okay," I say. "I'm offering this software not only to you or The Facts, Bernie, but to the whole world. We talked about it at HRS and decided that we didn't want to commercialize it. We believe that S3 is one of the things that can help to create a better world. And we also think that this software can help to accomplish just that. And that's why HRS makes it available in full and for free — to anyone who wants it."

"Really?" Bernie asks. He looks at Kate and me in disbelief.

"Yes, and probably even as an open source package. That way, those who want to can continue building and evolving it."

Bernie clearly doesn't know what to say. His eyes are moist and he looks at me, at Kate and back again.

"Thank you, Chris," he finally says. "This is the most beautiful gift that you could have given me."

"I thank you," I say as we give each other a big hug.

ACKNOWLEDGEMENTS

Writing this novel was a very instructive process. I generally derived more energy from it than it cost me, partly because of the incredible support I received from the universe and a number of people around me. And I would like to thank them here.

I'm tremendously thankful to James Priest, Bernhard Bockelbrink and Liliana David, the co-creators and co-developers of S3, for having brought S3 into the world. And for the opportunity to contribute, with them, my share to its further evolution.

I also want to thank Karen, my life partner, for the loving moral and practical support she gave me during the creation of this work.

This book and my passion for S3 would never have seen the light of day without the fertile ground that iLean and our clients and partners have been for me. It is fantastic to grow — together with my iLean friends and colleagues — our own consciousness and skills while contributing to creating more humane and effective organizations around us.

I originally wrote this book in Dutch, my mother tongue. I'm very grateful that Anita, who lives and breathes the S3 principles, was willing to do the initial translation of the manuscript to English. The feedback and suggestions I started receiving from James Priest so substantially improved the fluency, accuracy and depth of this novel that he rightly became the co-author of this book. Thanks so much for your time and dedication, James!

This story has gone through a number of versions. And it is, among others, due to the many proofreaders that this book has found its final form and quality. Thank you, Rob, Gina, Isabel, Vincent, Kari, John, Joost, Urs, Matthew, Samvel, Hugo and Bernhard. Thanks also to Niels, Mitchell, Gert, Anna and the team of LannooCampus for all the professional support.

And finally, I want to thank you, dear readers. Not only for reading this book, but above all for all the good you will do in the world by implementing S3 patterns.

Jef Cumps

WHAT IS SOCIOCRACY 3.0?

Collaborating more consciously and effectively on any scale!

Sociocracy 3.0 — or S3 in short — is a practical guide for creating and continuously evolving more agile, resilient and meaningful organizations. S3 successfully combines the principles of sociocratic thinking with the agile mindset and techniques. It offers teams and organizations a coherent way of growing towards a culture based on equivalence, accountability, effectiveness and continuous improvement.

What makes S3 so impactful is that it provides more than 70 immediately usable patterns, which can and should be implemented in a modular and flexible manner, based on actual needs. This way, S3 helps organizations to navigate through this complex world step by step, without major reorganizations or cumbersome transformation programs.

The co-creators of S3 consciously chose to make S3 available to the world for free via a Creative Commons license.

For more information about Sociocracy 3.0 see *www.sociocracy30.org.*

ABOUT THE AUTHOR / JEF CUMPS

After having completed his engineering studies in 2001, Jef started working as a developer in a small software company. That is where he joined an "agile" team and got used to an organizational culture that naturally combined caring about people with delivering great results.

Jef only fully grasped the power of these small, semi-autonomous teams after becoming a management consultant in a large, cumbersome organization. He has since made it his mission to bring new ways to look at work and organizations into the world. Further developing his inherent people skills by studying NLP, personal coaching, and leadership, and by developing his intuition helped him to become a solid coach and inspiring trainer.

About 10 years ago, Jef founded — together with some friends — the organization iLean. Initially, their objective was to help teams and organizations successfully implement Agile and Lean techniques. The focus later evolved toward supporting the often challenging organizational changes that go hand in hand with it. Today, iLean is a collective of experienced coaches and trainers who focus on supporting self-organization, effectiveness and agility on team and organizational level, as well as the leadership that comes with it. S3 plays a key role in this, both for iLean and for its clients.

Soon after the birth of S3, Jef became involved in further evolving and spreading it. He is one of the most experienced S3 coaches and trainers worldwide and a co-founder of learnS3.org.

Besides being a trainer, organizational coach and author, Jef is the partner of Karen and the proud father of Jannes and Toos.

Let's create a happy workplace!

Jef can be reached at *jef@ilean.be*. You can find more information about iLean on *www.ilean.be*, including the S3 workshops and courses hosted by Jef.

ABOUT THE CO-AUTHOR / JAMES PRIEST

James is a co-creator and co-developer of Sociocracy 3.0. He got together with Bernhard Bockelbrink in 2014 to experiment with synergies between sociocratic and agile principles and practices. They co-created and launched the first iteration of S3 in 2015 in response to a growing desire from people in organizations to preserve their humanity while scaling agility beyond operations to business wide. Liliana David joined the team soon after and the three of them work together developing S3 and providing free learning resources to the community.

James first discovered and experimented with the Sociocratic Circle-Organization Method in 2001. He was immediately excited about the potential of sociocratic thinking to help people transcend the limitations of a binary worldview and intentionally distribute power in healthy ways to better navigate complexity. Today he combines his extensive experience of sociocracy with almost two decades of practice in the fields of holistic organizational development, facilitative leadership and personal and relational transformation across a variety of sectors from corporations, to social enterprises, non-profits, children and communities.

An advocate of life-long learning and practices for more conscious collaboration, he divides his time between family, developing S3 and going where he's invited to help people learn about Sociocracy 3.0 and help organizations to develop business wide agility.

James is the co-author of this book, providing technical editing to ensure that it's as accurate and up to date with S3 as possible.

You can reach James at *james@thriveincollaboration.com.* For more information about the S3 courses and services James provides, visit *www.thriveincollaboration.com.*

THE MOST IMPORTANT S3 PATTERNS